Jim Burke

Classroom Management

How to:
- Establish Positive Discipline
- Organize Your Classroom
- Manage Your Teaching Time

SCHOLASTIC

D0169839

Dedication:

To America's newest teachers

Editor: Lois Bridges

Copyeditor: Carol Ghiglieri

Cover and interior designer: Maria Lilja

Cover photo: Bruce Forrester

Interior photos: Bruce Forrester unless otherwise indicated.

ISBN 13: 978-0-439-93446-6

ISBN 10: 0-439-93446-X

Contents

Introduction 5

Classroom Management Self-Assessment 8

Your Classroom

1. Create a Positive First Impression 10

2. Maintain a Positive and Productive
   Relationship With All Students 15

3. Use Your Walls to Educate, Communicate,
   and Celebrate 21

4. Assign Seats Based on Individual
   and Instructional Needs 27

Effective Instruction

1. Begin the Period Efficiently 32

2. End the Period Productively 37

3. Provide a Disciplined, Supportive
   Classroom Environment 41

4. Manage Group Instruction Productively 47

Learning for All 52

1. Meet the Needs of All Students 52

2. Meet the Needs of English Language Learners 57

3. Support Students With Special Needs 62

4. Support Students With Specific
   Learning Disabilities 68

Positive Discipline

Positive Discipline 74

1. Teach Self-Discipline and Personal Responsibility 74
2. Administer Discipline With Dignity 80
3. Communicate Policies, Procedures, and Principles in Your Syllabus 85
4. Establish and Maintain an Effective Approach to Discipline 90

Troubleshooting

1. Assignments 95
2. Attendance 97
3. Record Keeping 98
4. Abuse 100
5. Cheating 102
6. Materials and Equipment 104
7. Field Trips 105
8. Substitutes 106
9. Emergencies 108
10. Conferences 109

Recommended Reading 112

Introduction

The *Teacher's Essential Guide to Classroom Management* offers you concise, effective solutions to the most common instructional challenges all teachers face. These solutions are based on a combination of research and my own experience as a public school teacher who, like you, gets up every morning and teaches kids. It is this experience in the classroom that reminds me daily how little time we have to do the professional reading we wish we could and know we must do if we are

to improve. I've written this book with teachers like us in mind, striving to create a truly helpful book that is small enough to keep in your desk or carry in your pocket.

This book has a number of key features designed to help you learn at the speed of need:

- A self-assessment to help you identify those areas you want to improve and key ideas to help you develop a personal improvement plan to address those areas.

- Short chapters that each focus on a crucial aspect of classroom management.

- Guiding principles for each aspect of classroom management anchored in research and practical experience.

- In each chapter you'll find extra help for new teachers labeled "New Teacher Notes," as well as "Legal Notes," and a "Keep in Mind" box that calls attention to cultural diversity and sensitivity issues.

- A troubleshooting section that offers targeted solutions to specific problems nearly every teacher encounters with classroom management.

- Carefully chosen recommended readings for those who wish to examine certain subjects in greater depth.

Classroom management consistently ranks among the top challenges faced by all teachers but especially new teachers. Many potentially great teachers leave the profession because they were never taught how to guide and govern—how to lead that wonderful, restless bunch of kids we call a class. It is also important for a very obvious reason: nothing else can happen in the room if the class is not prepared to learn. Classroom management is about not only creating an effective classroom environment but also reducing your stress, increasing your students' productivity, and ensuring a safe, equitable environment.

Bob Daemmrich/The Image Works

I am grateful for the chance to share with you what has worked for me. As is so often the case, my classes always seem larger than they should be, and students are rarely as eager to learn as I wish they were. Thus it is my job to find out how to light that learning fire and keep it alive within them. Writing this book has allowed me to reflect on my own practices while learning from others' as well. In this way, the book has helped guide me as I have sought to learn how to better manage my own classroom. I hope this book can also become your essential guide to managing your classroom.

Classroom Management Self-Assessment

For each of the items below, record an answer between 1 and 5.

1 Never	**2** Rarely	**3** Sometimes	**4** Usually	**5** Always

Classroom

☐ I create a positive first impression.

☐ I use my walls to educate, communicate, and celebrate.

☐ I arrange desks and assign seats based on individual and instructional needs.

☐ I develop and maintain a positive and productive relationship with all students.

Instruction

☐ I begin the period effectively.

☐ I end the period effectively.

☐ I provide a disciplined, supportive classroom environment.

☐ I use and manage group instruction productively.

Learning

☐ I strive to meet the needs of all students.

☐ I strive to meet the needs of English Learners.

☐ I strive to meet the special needs of students in my classes.

☐ I strive to meet the needs of students with specific learning needs.

Discipline

☐ I teach students self-discipline and personal responsibility.

☐ I administer discipline with dignity.

☐ I define and communicate policies, procedures, and principles in my syllabus.

☐ I establish and maintain effective discipline.

Troubleshooting

☐ My students do all their in-class and homework assignments.

☐ My students attend class regularly, arriving to class on time each day.

☐ Students do not experience any type of abuse in my classroom.

☐ My students do not cheat or plagiarize.

☐ I am prepared for and know what to do in the event of different types of emergencies.

☐ I have no problems taking students to the library, lab, or on field trips.

☐ I provide substitutes with the information and resources they need to be effective.

☐ I store, organize, and take care of all equipment and supplies.

☐ I keep track of and make effective use of student information.

☐ I come prepared to conferences with parents, students, administrators, or counselors.

After completing this self-assessment, identify those areas with most urgent need of attention and improvement. For each statement to which your response was "never," "rarely," or "sometimes," go to the corresponding chapter and learn what you can do to improve in that area.

Your Classroom

1. Create a Positive First Impression

Kids know almost immediately what they think about a class based on what they see, what the teacher asks them to do, and how that teacher acts. Within seconds, students form impressions and expectations about your competence, your attitude toward students, and the work they will do. As a teacher, you want students to leave eager to return, glad that they have an instructor who is professional, organized, and caring, but also fun and interesting. Beginning with that end in mind, you cannot leave crucial details to chance. You must plan carefully to create the first impression and solid start you need in order to achieve the end you want.

Guiding Principles

1. Establish expectations regarding behavior, culture, policies, and procedures right away.

2. Communicate and apply these expectations clearly and consistently.

3. Get to know each other through academic and social activities.

4. Create an environment that makes room for fun and comfort while emphasizing learning.

5. Dress, act, and speak like a caring, serious professional.

Index Open

Establish expectations regarding behavior, culture, policies, and procedures right way.

When you set boundaries you help students understand how the class works. Boundaries allow students to feel comfortable and safe, so they can focus on learning and enjoying the class. Here are some suggestions for setting the right tone in your class:

- Discuss and clarify policies with students regarding attendance, homework, electronic devices, missing work, and hall passes.

- Post policies and procedures in your classroom so that they are always available to your students and to you.

- Define consequences without making threats. Instead of saying "If you come to class late I will not accept your homework," say "I do not accept late homework."

- Assess students' understanding of the policies and procedures by creating a quiz.

- Practice what you preach by following your own policies and explaining reasons and consequences.

- Refine and reiterate expectations as each new semester begins. Keep what works for you, and jettison what doesn't.

Communicate and apply these expectations clearly and consistently.

The opening days define you as a teacher: what you do and say must agree, otherwise students will quickly learn not to trust your words. In those openings weeks:

- Begin each day by reviewing the relevant policies or procedures for class.

- Come prepared each day with challenging assignments that you can model and explain, thus demonstrating your commitment to each student's success in your class.

- Follow through on any policies regarding missing work or tardies from the first day. If, for example, you say you do not accept late work, make no exceptions beginning the first day.

- Recognize that new students must learn the ways of your class in particular and the school in general.

- Be regimented in how your class works, so students learn what to expect and how to satisfy those expectations.

> **New Teacher Note!** Be prepared to wear many hats. We teachers play many roles whether we want to or not, all of which begin that first day: teacher, mentor, leader, coach, guide, role model, and counselor.

Get to know each other through academic and social activities.

Some of students' most important first impressions revolve around whether or not they feel secure in your classroom. *Will I feel comfortable participating in discussions? Will anyone make fun of me? Will my opinion matter?* To achieve this trust, you have to give kids a chance to get to know each other and get to know something about themselves, too. Here are some ways to accomplish this:

- Write a letter to your class or send them each an e-mail.

Photos.com

- Have students decorate their binder for your class with images and words that are important to them. Then provide students time to share and discuss the binders as a way to introduce themselves to each other.

- Ask students to complete a student interest survey and then discuss their answers during class.

- Share something interesting about yourself, so they see you are willing to let them get to know you, too. Kids like to know that you race horses on weekends, and graduated from this school.

Student Interest Sample Questions

- Favorite activity online?
- Best place you've ever visited?
- Best book read?
- Other languages you speak?
- Extracurricular activities or sports?

Create a classroom environment that makes room for fun and comfort while emphasizing learning.

Incorporating humor and play into work inspires creativity and sustained interest in the work at hand. Most of us want our students to leave that first day having enjoyed a good laugh even as they began working with course content that reveals our high expectations and students' current level of knowledge. One person I know said that on the first day of class he would ask his teacher a question she wouldn't know the answer to; if she said she didn't know, he respected her; if she made up an answer, he made her life miserable for the rest of the year. Begin the year by trying to:

- Greet students as they come in, shaking their hand and asking their name.

- Display pictures from the previous year to share what happens in your class.

- Admit you don't know everything and are here to learn and have fun, too.

- Post your state, district, and school standards to emphasize high expectations.

- Display posters, proverbs, and images that inspire all students to succeed.

Dress, act, and speak like a caring, serious professional.

The most important daily test teachers must pass is the "dinner table test." Every day kids go home to parents who ask about their day in school. Everything we do or say as teachers should make sense to parents when they hear about it; otherwise we lose credibility in the eyes of our students and their parents. Cultivate this professional persona by paying attention to the following:

- Dress in a way that inspires confidence in you and your teaching. This could mean a jacket and tie, or a dress, but it should always be appropriate for work.

- Speak in a positive, supportive way without trying to be one of the kids. You are there to lead and teach them; they are your students, not your friends.

- Be in class on time and ready to go when the bell rings, so students see that the class has important work to do and that you have come prepared to teach.

- Never talk disparagingly about other classes, students, teachers, or administrators from the past or the present.

- Avoid sarcasm or other ways of embarrassing and humiliating students, such as singling out students.

- Be a role model and a professional: everything you do teaches your students.

2. Maintain a Positive and Productive Relationship With All Students

The student-teacher relationship is the cornerstone of an engaging, successful classroom. Everyone works better for someone they respect and enjoy, and both teachers and students will do their best if they invest in this relationship. You must provide the leadership in this crucial area, for you cannot expect students to enter your class knowing how to manage their relationships with you. In addition to being a leader and counselor, coach and mentor, you must be, of course, a *teacher* who works likea a *gardener*. That is, you must prepare the soil, providing a rich, nurturing environment in which all your students will grow and thrive despite their different needs.

Guiding Principles

1. Establish and maintain a professional relationship with your students.

2. Set high expectations and help students reach them.

3. Show a personal interest in your students in and outside of school.

4. Treat all students with respect and consideration.

5. Listen to and learn from students but lead based on your own judgment.

Establish and maintain a professional relationship with your students.

As a teacher, you are not your students' friend nor are you their parent. You are the adult charged with the task of shaping students into capable, confident adults. Likewise, students are not your customers, nor are they your own children. Think of it this way: students are the players you have to coach into a team of successful individuals. To create this relationship you need to:

- Address students in a warm but appropriate tone in class and around school.

- Provide professional guidance but not personal intimacy.

- Make yourself available to students who see you as a personal mentor or academic guide.

- Ask students to address you appropriately in and outside of class.

- Recognize the absolute importance of personal and legal boundaries.

New Teacher Note! Students are easily influenced and quick to devote themselves to teachers who take an active interest in them. Avoid even well-intended physical affection or emotional intimacy with students that could cause confusion and even cost you your job.

Set high expectations and help students reach them.

Meaningful, purposeful work that challenges students is fundamental to a strong teacher-student relationship. In the absence of work that engages them, students will resist and ultimately resent the teacher, seeing the class as a waste of time. Such disengagement increases the likelihood of disruption which can undermine the larger momentum of the class as a whole. To avoid such situations, consider the following:

- Demonstrate your high expectations through the intellectual and creative challenge of the work, not the amount of it.

- Create assignments that challenge students to work above but not beyond their current instructional level.

- Connect what students are doing to subsequent classes, college, and the workplace to reinforce its value and purpose. I tell my students, for example, that the ability to communicate effectively and take tests often determine who gets a job or promotion. Our local fire department received 5,000 applications for one opening, then reduced it to fifty by giving two tests, one multiple choice, the other written.

- Demonstrate how to do the assigned work so students see what a successful performance on this challenging material looks like.

- Meet with students who need additional help to show you care and to ensure their success.

Show a personal interest in your students in and outside of school.

Kids want to know that you think of them as more than a grade and a student ID number. For some kids, teachers are the most important adults in their lives, a huge responsibility to juggle given all your pressing academic and professional demands. A course, a semester, even a few years at a certain school, is such a thin slice of each student's life. However, when you know what kids do and what their interests are outside of school, you can use that information in class to make connections that will help students enjoy what is taught in school and motivate them to learn. Here are some suggestions for how to connect with your students:

- Gather information about students' interests through assignments, surveys, and conversations.

- Talk with kids in the minutes before class begins, asking about their participation in upcoming school events or extracurricular activities.

- Add appropriate personal notes on student papers, focusing on the personal and academic growth you observe in the paper.

- Alert students to events, activities, and opportunities you know might interest them.

- Incorporate activities, subjects, and texts that you know will interest students.

Keep in Mind Some cultures have strict customs regarding how children should interact with adults, especially those outside the family or in positions of authority, such as teachers.

Treat all students with respect and consideration.

Teachers cannot help but bring their own biases and attitudes to the classroom; yet we must strive to leave them outside, checking them at the door. So, regardless of your private opinions about immigration, religion, politics, culture, intelligence—or anything else, really—you must enter the classroom prepared to do all you can for *all* who enter. Whereas Dante's *Inferno* boasts a sign over the gate of Hell that reads, "Abandon all hope ye who enter here," the classroom door must be a portal of hope for all who walk through it. To create such an environment you can:

- Monitor your language and behavior for bias or attitude based on appearance, status, or performance.

- Evaluate what you say and how you act for "micro-agression," little jabs and punches that emotionally bruise, humiliate, or isolate students.

- Solicit students' thoughts and feelings about the class and show, through your actions, that you listened to and will address their concerns and needs.

Maria Lilja

- Encourage all students to participate in class discussions and activities, preparing them to succeed and praising their contributions.

- Avoid sarcasm or other humiliating language at all times, even when you are "just kidding." Here's a rule of thumb: do not make any remarks that you might feel you should follow up by saying, "Just kidding!"

Listen to and learn from students but lead based on your own judgment.

Students expect teachers to be authoritative but not authoritarian. They want to know that as the adult you have a firm hand on the rudder and will steer the class to the right destination. Still, they also expect you to listen to them if they have valid remarks about how to improve the class in general or an assignment in particular. Everyone wants a leader who is firm *and* fair. To accomplish this balanced leadership, you can:

- Ask students for feedback on assignments, requesting ways you can improve a specific assignment or aspects of your instruction in general. Often, at the end of a big assignment, I will ask students to tell me what was difficult and what I did that helped. I typically ask, on new assignments, how I could improve it next time.

- Thank the class for the new insights they have given you, specifically mentioning those aspects of instruction you will work to improve as a result of their feedback.

- Write the class a letter outlining what has been going well and what needs improvement. Then explain what you will be changing and how you think those changes will help students all learn and enjoy the class more.

- Take students seriously. Provide a daily model of the Golden Rule while realizing that this is a rule they are still learning to live by.

3. Use Your Walls to Educate, Communicate, and Celebrate

Walls are like storefronts given to teachers. Use them to advertise your products (what you teach) and inform your public (your students) about upcoming events and important information. Every item on the walls of your room should serve a purpose. Some material on the walls, such as an emergency plan and procedure chart, is general and mandatory; other information, like announcements or vocabulary words, is specific to your classroom. Both types work to create a first impression in the students' minds, suggesting that this teacher is (or is *not*) organized, professional, and committed to student success in and outside of class. Just as people know upon entering a store whether they trust the goods, so, too, do students enter your classroom, judging from what they see on the walls whether they will buy what you are selling.

Guiding Principles

1. Use the walls to teach and reinforce key content and skills.

2. Showcase student work on the walls.

3. Communicate essential information on a dedicated bulletin board.

4. Share the walls with your students so the classroom is "our" space not "your" space.

5. Extend your walls to include digital spaces.

Use the walls to teach and reinforce key content and skills.

Too often, important content appears on our overhead projectors or our whiteboards only to vanish at the end of the period. When we do this our lessons can become singular episodes all too easily forgotten or left behind. That's why it's so important to use your room to extend and reinforce your teaching. Display your student's learning through posters, bulletin boards, and extra whiteboards. To this end you can post:

- Key test-taking strategies.

- A model of the reading process or reminders of what effective readers do.

- A poster with questions students should ask themselves during the writing process.

- Strategies to use in solving problems or doing experiments.

- Useful information about grammar, usage, or mechanics.

- Sample sentence starters to use when writing.

- Useful vocabulary related to current lesson.

I KNOW I'M STUCK
AS A READER WHEN...

- I find myself "fake reading"
- I start daydreaming / get distracted
- I get sleepy / bored / don't feel interested
- I can't retell what I've read
- I feel like I'm missing something / the parts don't seem to fit together
- I find myself skipping parts
- The "voice in my head" is silent or just says things like "Huh?"
- I can't create a picture in my head
- I have too many questions + not enough answers or clues
- I feel I have to keep reading the same part over + over
- I find myself reading the same part over + over without making progress
- I come across too many words I don't know

Showcase student work on the walls.

Schools line the halls with trophy cases to show their pride in all the students have achieved; shouldn't classrooms do the same? Such a question invites you to reflect on what you are having kids do that might inspire pride and be worthy of display. Try the following suggestions:

- Post model papers or other assignments that celebrate students' work while also showing others what a successful assignment or project looks like.

- Mount a large common project such as a quilt or table of elements, each square of which is done by a different student and represents a different part of the larger idea.

- Arrange visual or graphic displays of processes, procedures, or stories.

- Feature models that represent key concepts or themes in the course or its texts.

Keep in Mind Include compelling quotations and images of men and women from different cultures on your bulletin boards. Students should see themselves reflected in your classroom.

> **New Teacher Note!** Consider having a dedicated bulletin board that features all required information. Administrators often look for it when they visit to observe or evaluate your classes.

Communicate essential information on a dedicated bulletin board.

Certain state laws and evacuation procedures must, by law, be prominently posted, often in multiple languages. Others are not mandatory but are expected. For example, your district may require the posting of content standards. In that case, write the standards you are covering that day on the board up front. Schools committed to school-wide reform or instructional practices might require you to post a list describing the core instructional practices for all to see. In addition, you might:

- Show class and/or school calendars and bell schedules where all can see them.

- Post emergency evacuation information.

- Highlight school bulletins and announcements about upcoming events.

- Announce scholarship, volunteer, and other opportunities on a special bulletin board for news and announcements.

- Display school policies regarding dress codes, weapons, plagiarism, electronic devices, and drugs.

Share the walls with your students so the classroom is "our" space not "your" space.

Some teachers make their room into a living museum, covering the walls with posters, photographs, headlines, and artifacts from science, history, or literature. The room seems to burst with color and energy when kids first walk into it. However, research finds that kids connect more to a classroom where there is space for their work and interests; otherwise they come to feel like they are in a museum with a big "Do Not Touch!" sign. Remember, the space you dedicate to the kids doesn't have to be huge. Here are some ideas you may want to consider:

- Create a bulletin board called "Our Space" as a positive alternative to the Web site MySpace.com.

- Post big sheets of paper on which kids can write their own thoughts about the subject you are studying.

- Have students create their own posters and artifacts, using yours as models.

- Dedicate a space for students to post fliers for clubs, announcements for upcoming performances, or times for study groups to meet.

Extend your walls to include digital spaces.

As schools become more digital, the boundaries of our classrooms also extend beyond the physical walls. Schools all have Web sites now, and increasingly teachers have their own sites. Still, many teachers and schools are trying to make sense of how to use these digital spaces to communicate, educate, and celebrate. Here are a few things you might try, all of which are available through such online services as Schoolloop.com, powerschool.com, and Scholastic.com:

- Post your syllabus, guidelines, and other important documents on your class Web site.

- Post your homework assignment on the Web site or through e-mail.

- Provide an opportunity for students to comment on books, ideas, or experiments through online threaded discussions.

- Send e-mails out to the whole class through a listserv with praise for work done or reminders of upcoming due dates or events.

- Have your class create its own Web page on which they can publish their work for others to see.

- Create a digital textbook with links to specific resources as I did on my Web site (www.englishcompanion.com).

4. Assign Seats Based on Individual and Instructional Needs

Students base much of their first impression on how your room appears and is arranged. (Of course, many teachers do not have their own room; many "travel" between classes, leaving them little choice in arrangement and less room for storage than others.) Some of the factors that affect seat arrangement and assignment: shape of the room, size of the desks, number of students, type of class, religious customs, and instructional needs as mandated by special accommodation plans. We always seem to be trying to fit more—more content, equipment, students, materials—into less time and space. Where students sit and the arrangement of those seats determine how students will work and contribute to the safety and efficiency of the class, so it's important to get it right. Consider the following when determining how to arrange and assign students seats:

Guiding Principles

1. Consider students' individual needs.

2. Arrange desks to maximize use of the space.

3. Configure desks for effectiveness, efficiency, and flexibility.

4. Locate equipment, materials, and work stations for easy access, viewing, and use.

5. Create and maintain an updated seating chart.

Consider students' individual needs.

Some students enter our classes with mandated needs, such as sitting near the front of the class. Some even have aides who must sit near or with them. Or a Muslim girl, on the other hand, often may prefer to not sit near boys. The only way we can meet these needs is to get to know our students, which means gathering information from them immediately about what they need to succeed. Here are some suggestions:

- Distribute a student information survey as soon as possible to gather essential information that will help you determine the right arrangement and placement for each student.

- Read the Individual Education Program (IEP) for any special-education students.

- Identify any student with special needs regarding vision, environmental distractions, language, or culture. Assign seats and make accommodations accordingly.

New Teacher Note! Special education accommodations are legally binding, so be sure to know and meet these needs. Seating arrangement is often a key element of a student's education plan.

Arrange desks to maximize use of the space.

Few rooms are used for one purpose only. Most teachers have at least two different classes, which may have competing needs. The senior teacher with 35 Advanced Placement students might also teach a couple sections of reading to freshmen; thus the room must serve a range of needs. Think about the following when arranging your room:

- Determine your primary instructional space and organize the room around it.

- Place stations, centers, or tables on the periphery.

- Check sight lines to ensure that all students can see the board clearly.

- Remove extra desks and unnecessary furniture or equipment.

Configure desks for effectiveness, efficiency, and flexibility.

Consider the "verbs" that will characterize what students do in your class; that is, what actions will students do in the room: *confer, collaborate, construct, experiment, read*? What arrangement best suits those different actions? Try the following when configuring your desks:

- Determine which arrangement is most effective for your subject and instruction.

- Consider your instructional methods (e.g., lecture, demonstration, groups) and the means (e.g., whiteboard,

Smartboard, computer with LCD, overhead, lab stations, computer stations) you will use.

- Choose a seating arrangement that allows students to move quickly in and out of a variety of configurations (e.g., full-class lecture, pairs, groups, literature circles).

- Evaluate the safety of your seating arrangement: Can all students evacuate quickly and safely in the event of an emergency?

- Place your own desk on the basis of how you will use it to store materials, meet with students, do your own work, or monitor the class as they work or take tests.

Keep in Mind Students from some countries or cultures bring specific needs to class regarding where and with whom they sit. Bear this in mind when assigning seats.

Locate equipment, materials, and work stations for easy access, viewing, and use.

Most classes come with a wide assortment of books, materials, and equipment to work with in various instructional contexts. Plan accordingly with the following in mind:

- Place any equipment that will distract or pose a hazard outside of the primary instructional area.

- Arrange textbooks and related reference materials near the door for easy access as students come in; direct them to grab a book or handouts as they enter.

- Put study centers, computer stations, or teacher conference areas where they will provide the most privacy and least distraction to others.

Create and maintain an updated seating chart.

Seating charts are essential tools to help you solve a range of organizational, behavioral, and instructional problems. They are also crucial when you have a substitute or are beginning a new semester. Try these different approaches to using a seating chart:

- Create an alphabetical seating chart for the first day based on your class roster and use that until you better understand your students' specific needs.

- Make multiple copies of your seating chart so you can use them for different purposes (e.g., keeping track of participation, taking roll, assigning groups).

- Provide a current copy of your seating chart to all substitutes with assurances that it is, in fact, current.

- Format your seating chart to allow room to make notes regarding participation, IEP accommodations, or other important reminders.

- Write students' names on small sticky notes or create seating charts using a computer program to allow for easy rearrangement.

- Reassign seats, that is "shuffle the deck," periodically so students meet and learn to work with as many people as possible.

Effective Instruction

1. Begin the Period Efficiently

Every new period is like a story: it must have a beginning, middle, and an end, while developing meaningful themes as it unfolds. The beginning minutes are crucial to your own success as well as that of your class, for you have to get a great deal done in those few minutes if the period is to become a memorable story. Within those opening minutes, you must accomplish a range of social, logistical, administrative, and, of course, instructional goals, as your new group of students are settling into the classroom. Luckily, things usually end as well as they begin, so here's what you can do to get each class off to a great start every day.

Guiding Principles

1. Use the time before class begins to set up your lesson and greet your students.

2. Take care of logistical and administrative details at the very beginning of class.

3. Create and maintain a flexible routine for beginning class.

4. Communicate to students what they will do and how they will do it.

5. Begin class with a warm-up activity that sets the tone and prepares students to learn.

Use the time before class begins to set up your lesson and greet your students.

While most Broadway productions do one show a day, teachers do five or even six. Each one requires us to set up equipment, gather supplies, have handouts ready, and get essential information on the board. Even more challenging, we only have a few minutes between classes to get it done. At the same time, kids are streaming into class, and need to talk about academic and personal issues. During this time before class, you might try to accomplish the following:

- Write the homework assignment and other important information for the day on the board.

- Set up any equipment—DVDs, LCDs, lab equipment, overhead projector—so it is ready to go at the bell.

- Write an outline of your instructional goals on the board.

- Check with students about missing work or other academic concerns.

- Mingle with your students. Whenever possible, greet them by name, wave, smile at specific students as they enter. If you know Jeanne had a championship game the previous day, go ask her how it went. If John shows up after being absent, ask how he is, remind him to see you about missed work.

New Teacher Note! Use the first 5–10 minutes to have students do an academic warm-up or quick review so you have a chance to prepare for the main activity.

Take care of logistical and administrative details at the very beginning of class.

Between announcements and roll call, summons notes and chit-chat, there is plenty to undermine an effective beginning to a class. As Colin Powell once said though, "Success is never an accident but the result of careful planning." You must be ready to begin efficiently so that you can accomplish all that you must. Here's what you need to accomplish:

- Take roll by whatever system your school uses.

- Make any announcements related to your class or school in general.

- Point out the homework on the board, reminding students to write it down before the end of the period.

- Tell kids where to sit or how to prepare for the work they will do that day.

- Collect any documents, such as permission slips, while taking roll.

- Record tardies by having late students sign in on a clipboard.

Create and maintain a flexible routine for beginning class.

While variation is a human need, so is structure. Students, especially those new to the class or those with special needs, benefit tremendously from a predictable environment. It helps them understand how to behave, what to have on hand, and where to go. In the absence of structure, students develop patterns that are counterproductive for themselves and the class. Try this to help them stay on track:

- Begin with an activity for the first 5–10 minutes that serves as a transition from students' last class.

- Check notebooks or confer with students about papers or projects while they do the opening activity.

- Dedicate specific activities on specific days—e.g., quizzes on Thursdays, academic workout on Monday, Wednesday, and Friday—so students come in knowing what to expect.

- Have a different student each day deliver the minutes describing what the class did the previous day.

Legal Note! Keep careful records for attendance as these are legal documents that can have real consequences—for you and students—if they are not complete and accurate.

Communicate to students what they will be doing and how they will do it.

Students walk into each class wondering, often aloud, "Are we going to be doing anything important today?" Upon entering, students need to find a teacher who knows what the class is doing and creates a sense of mission to accomplish it. Here are some steps toward clear communication:

- List the key ideas you expect students to learn on the board.

- Write an outline schedule of what students will do in class that day.

- Above all, tell students what to do, how to do it, and why they are doing or learning it.

- Distribute handouts that explain and support what they will do that day.

- Create in your class a sense of urgency by emphasizing the importance of the work. I often say, for example, "We have important work to get to, so we need to get this first step done well but fast, so we can get to the main course of today's meal."

Begin class with a warm-up activity that sets the tone and prepares students to learn.

Use the first 5–10 minutes to get students mentally warmed up, intellectually engaged, or emotionally connected to the content that will make up the "main course" of the period for the other 40 minutes. This anticipatory set helps them activate background knowledge, as well as reflect on their past experiences with and feelings about the day's subject. It also serves as a transition from the previous class. During this time, you can accomplish the other things you need to attend to such as taking attendance. Possible opening activities include having students:

- Write in their journals in response to an essential question or take down information from the board they will need to use in class that day.

- Engage in a daily "academic workout" on a specific aspect of vocabulary, writing, or mathematics.

- Read a text selection they will use in class that day.

- Ask students to present on news topics, vocabulary, or what the class did the day before.

- Read aloud from a supplementary text that deepens their learning.

Maria Lilja

2. End the Period Productively

Ernest Hemingway advised fellow writers to stop writing for the day when they knew exactly what the next line would be. Hemingway's advice reminds us of the narrative aspect of our work, the way one day connects to the next and, if we are lucky, becomes part of one long story of all that we learned and did during that year together. Like writers, teachers have so many things going on, all of which we must bring to some coherent closure at the end—not an easy task when it involves as many as 40 different students. Yet within these closing minutes, you must not only end the current period but be sure students know what to do for the next one. Students also need to know what the homework is, how to do it, and how it will prepare them for the next day's class.

Guiding Principles

1. Establish and maintain a flexible but predictable routine.

2. Restore the classroom to its original order.

3. Use the final minutes to reflect, review, assess, or discuss.

4. Take care of essential procedural details in an orderly way.

5. Assign and explain the homework for that night.

Establish and maintain a flexible but predictable routine.

What matters most is that kids know what to expect and know that their needs will be met before the bell. Students have a variety of emotional and educational needs in the final minutes. Consider the following to ensure an effective ending to the period:

- End by the bell so students will have time to get to their next class.

- Post on the board what needs to be done by the end of the period each day.

- Dedicate certain tasks or activities on specific days at the end of the period.

- Plan for the period to end with just enough time to accomplish all you must.

- Have an emergency plan for those days when you end early: a book to read aloud, an article to share, an image to put up and discuss, a fun but quick game to play or puzzle to solve.

Restore the classroom to its original order.

Active learning is often going to resemble what some call "managed chaos." During a given period, desks and tables might be moved all over, supplies scattered across tabletops, and chairs may end up in disarray. Before the bell rings, the classroom needs to be restored to its original order if you are to be ready for the next class. It works best to call people by name to do specific tasks. I'll say, "Hey, Jim, Greg, and Alan, I need you guys to move the table back, please. Eugene, grab a chair and put it where it belongs. Thanks, guys!" Here are a few suggestions for ending your class smoothly and efficiently:

- Create a big poster-size checklist with different roles and responsibilities you can assign to students each day or each week.

- Return all desks and chairs to their original positions.

- Place all materials and supplies back where they belong.

- Store all tools and equipment in the designated areas.

- Account for all checked-out equipment, books, or supplies.

New Teacher Note! Maintain strict order at the end of the period, particularly as it relates to students being out of their seats and gathering around the classroom door, before the bell.

Use the final minutes to reflect, review, assess, or discuss.

The final minutes offer an important opportunity to assess students' understanding of the content covered that day, or extend it through discussion. On some days it might be best to reflect on the process students used to solve problems, while on others it might be more appropriate to determine how well they understand the material. Such discussions or informal assessments might reveal gaps in their knowledge that suggest they are not prepared to do the assigned homework yet or that you need to plan class the next day to address those gaps. Try these suggestions for making the most of those final minutes:

- Complete an "exit card" on which students identify three key points about the day's lesson. They can hand it to you as they exit the class.

- Reflect on the process they used to arrive at their solutions and how it did or did not help.

- Give students a short quiz targeted at the key points you taught that day.

> **Sample Exit Card**
>
> Summary is:
> - in your own words
> - shorter than original text
> - useful way to better understand what you read

- Pose (or redirect students' attention back to) an essential question and use this as the basis for discussion or written reflection.

- Generate questions to consider about the day's topic when class resumes the following day.

Take care of essential procedural details in an orderly way.

Just as there are important procedures at the beginning of the period, so there are at the end. Unlike those at the beginning, however, these tend not to be mandatory; instead, these are essential to the effectiveness of any instruction and to the classroom environment. Consider the following procedures for your class:

- Collect work completed during the period, reminding students to put their name on it.

- Request or distribute such items as permission slips and other school documents.

- Sign or complete students' progress reports or other forms they may have.

- Ask students to turn in homework you may not have collected at the beginning.

- Update your roll book if students came in late and were marked absent.

> **Keep in Mind** In the rush of ending the period, it is easy to speak fast and forget that not everyone is fluent in English. Check with your English language learners to be sure they understand the homework assignment.

Assign and explain the homework for that night.

It is essential to provide time to go over the homework assignment so that students leave knowing what to do and when it is due. The whirlwind of the last minutes can easily undermine this process, forcing you to shout the homework over everyone's head. This, understandably, results in fewer completed assignments and little learning. The following are tips for assigning homework:

- Write the homework on the board, breaking it down into discrete steps for clarity.

- Have students get out their assignment sheets or planners to write it down.

- Explain each point thoroughly, providing examples and answering questions if necessary.

- Clarify your expectations regarding the quality and due date of the homework.

- Remind students that the homework is also online, if you or your school has a Web site.

3. Provide a Disciplined, Supportive Classroom Environment

An effective classroom environment provides not only the security but the support needed to do challenging work. Within a supportive, structured environment, students engage in work that has personal meaning and public value; that is, the work addresses students' need for personal exploration that leads to a sense of self but also provides them with the skills that will allow them to prosper in subsequent classes and the world beyond school. *Disciplined* does not need to imply "strict" so much as an environment that works well, one that is balanced between flexibility and accountability, creativity and productivity. It is your role as teacher to foster such a culture of quality; it is everyone's responsibility to maintain it by upholding the principles that govern such a classroom community.

Guiding Principles

1. Promote a strong work ethic within your classroom.

2. Cultivate and emphasize adaptability in your students.

3. Establish and maintain high expectations for all students on all assignments.

4. Develop a thoughtful, reflective classroom environment.

5. Foster a spirit of collaboration and support within your classroom.

Promote a strong work ethic within your classroom.

Students will not work hard if they see the work as meaningless or success as unattainable. They must believe that the work we ask them to do will bring the desired results. Moreover, many must learn what today's quick-fix culture does not always convey: hard work is an essential element of success in any endeavor. Such work inspires in students a faith in their ability to succeed, which translates into the effort needed to achieve that same success. This motivation must, in the long run, come from within, though you can nurture it in the supportive, disciplined environment of your classroom. To cultivate this work ethic, try the following:

- Show students you are willing to work just as hard and learn what you must to help them solve difficult problems. I'm happy to tell students I stayed up late trying to figure out what a poem meant.

- Ask students to identify what they already know or need to learn to be able to succeed at a specific assignment or task.

- Connect what students don't want to learn with what they do want to know in order to increase motivation. In algebra, for example, explain that it is algebraic equations that allow sound to be compressed into MP3 format for their iPods.

- Build a culture within the classroom that celebrates and respects working hard to solve problems and overcome challenges.

New Teacher Note! Teach yourself early on to believe that all students can succeed if given the skills and knowledge they need.

Cultivate and emphasize adaptability in your students.

Students live in a constantly changing world that asks them to work with people from different backgrounds, with different strengths, in situations that are not always controlled or comfortable. They must learn to navigate that complexity, finding and using their strengths along the way, and considering social and intellectual problems from different perspectives, not all of which may be familiar to them. The world expects them to be flexible, able to adapt their skills and knowledge to a given situation, one that might resist their initial efforts and demand from them creativity and persistence. You can instill in them this attitude and set of skills by doing the following:

- Cultivate an environment that values risk-taking and creativity as students consider subjects and solve problems from different perspectives using a variety of techniques.

- Provide an atmosphere of humor and security, fun and playfulness in which students can take the risks necessary to develop flexibility in their thinking.

- Provide opportunities for students to work with different media, configurations, or methods, and convey their results using those means that emphasize their strengths but also develop their weaknesses.

- Require students to consider the same problem from different perspectives, solve it using alternative strategies, and arrive at a result after you have added new complexities or data they must incorporate into their solution.

- Foster an atmosphere of uncertainty essential to authentic inquiry and guide students through it until they arrive at their own solution. For example, tell physics students they must create a vehicle powered only by a mousetrap, but leave the solution to them, offering suggestions only as needed, making solving the problem fun for them.

Establish and maintain high expectations for all students on all assignments.

Research on effective, high-performing classrooms consistently identifies a culture of high expectations as a determining factor in the success of students, particularly those who have not met the standards in the past. Such a culture of quality plays on the positive side of peer pressure. The message in such classrooms is *In here, it's cool to have ideas, to be smart, to work hard, and do well.* These expectations must come not only from you but from the students themselves. In this as in so many other areas, as the teacher you are the leader, the one who sets the tone, who provides the example for the students to follow. As many studies have found, the quality of the teacher—his or her expectations, skills, and knowledge—is the most important factor in improving student performance. You can create such a culture within your class if you:

- Establish a culture of high expectations early on by using examples, language, and assignments that challenge students not just to work hard but also think hard.

- Promote a productive level of dissatisfaction in their performance that suggests they can always do better, that "good enough" is not good enough.

- Set goals and devise steps students can follow to reach those goals, including gathering and reflecting on data about their performance or behavior.

- Emphasize high standards both in process and product, allowing students to revise or otherwise improve their performance using feedback from you or their peers.

- Help students internalize these high expectations for themselves and those with whom they work through reflection on and comments about their performance.

Keep in Mind Don't let yourself make assumptions about how students should do based on their culture. It is your job to create a culture for all students that emphasizes effort over ability when it comes to learning and success.

Develop a thoughtful, reflective classroom environment.

Only by thinking about what does and does not work can we better understand our own process and performance. Such a habit of reflection does not happen in the classroom on its own, however; it is the result of you creating time for and emphasizing the value of such thinking. This metacognitive awareness can, depending on your objectives, include not only the process but the product—not only what the students did but how they did it, why they did it, and how it felt to do it. In short, the reflective classroom makes room for questions about what did and did not work this time and how you can adjust your performance to improve next time. Here are some techniques you can try:

- Reflect on current or previous performances to determine what worked and why and how that knowledge can inform future performance.

- Develop useful questions students can ask about their emotional and cognitive processes, then post these on the classroom wall for easy reference and repeated use. *What strategies or questions did I use? How did that help?*

- Cite examples of successful people, such as athletes, who constantly reflect on their performance and use that information to improve. Wilt Chamberlain, for example, rated his performance after every game on a scale of 1–5, almost never giving himself a score above a 3!

- Provide students time and guidance to reflect on not only their individual performance but their group and the class as a whole.

- Help students identify emotional and cognitive patterns that affect their performance, and develop strategies for new, more productive processes.

Foster a spirit of collaboration and support within the classroom.

Today's workplace expects people from different backgrounds and with different skills to be able to work together to solve complex problems. Most industries now emphasize collaboration, asking people to work in teams, whether in sales, production, design, or management. A collaborative classroom not only develops social skills but improves students' ability to solve problems in concert with others, allowing them to focus on what they do well. Here are some ways to further enhance the collaborative culture of your classroom:

- Organize activities around different roles that allow students to contribute based on their strengths. If, for example, a project requires the creation of a movie or art work, help groups identify the students with those strengths.

- Provide opportunities within assignments for students to share what they know or help others solve a common problem.

- Bring questions to the class that you yourself do not know how to answer, in order to create a sense of working together to answer the big questions.

- Allow students to choose those roles or aspects of a project that interest them the most so they will engage with and contribute to the class. Literature circles, for example, provide a range of different roles, each of which plays to a different strength.

- Design opportunities for online collaboration, taking advantage (e.g., through threaded discussions) of students' interest in technology.

Maria Lilja

4. Manage Group Instruction Productively

Group work has a positive effect on student learning and performance; it increases engagement and comprehension, and improves students' attitudes toward the class and material. Groups allow students to learn from and ensure the success of others—but only if the activities are carefully organized and students are prepared for the work. Groups come in a variety of sizes: the full class, large groups (5–8), medium-size teams (3–4), and pairs. Whether a full class of kids or a pair of students, groups benefit most from orchestrated activities that have a clear objective so that everyone in the group has purposeful work to do, a clearly defined role to play. In the increasingly global, diverse, collaborative environment of the modern workplace, students must be able to work with others to solve different types of problems.

Guiding Principles

1. Provide the necessary conditions for effective group work.

2. Use a variety of ways of configuring groups to solve instructional problems.

3. Model and teach the appropriate behaviors and skills for successful group work.

4. Make effective transitions and maintain momentum during group instruction.

5. Monitor and provide feedback on group and individual performance.

Maria Lilja

Provide the necessary conditions for effective group work.

Several factors affect group work: class size, student needs, available time, and the demands of the task. Some of us teach English and lab classes with 45 students; others teach in schools or programs that enjoy class sizes under 20. The ability of the group to function well is also influenced by who is in a group and the environment in which that group works. Consider the following when preparing for group work:

- Create a sense of urgency by limiting the time students have to complete the task; you can add more time later if necessary. I usually say something like, "Okay, in three minutes I want each group to be ready to explain why..."

- Arrange the workspace so everyone has a place and can work productively. I have a big table where some can work; others organize themselves into clusters of desks. If we all need tables, I usually reserve the library, which has big tables.

- Assign students to groups based on their needs and the needs of the group.

- Establish clear guidelines and procedures for who does what, how it should be done, and when the assignment is due.

New Teacher Note! Avoid using groups as a default strategy for everything, especially when kids urge you to let them work together because "we work better when we work in groups." Use groups as an instructional solution.

Use a variety of ways of configuring groups to solve instructional problems.

Each group configuration or technique is a solution to a different problem; as with tools, your job is to choose the right one for the task. If you just want kids to compare their thinking with another's, students should work in pairs. If students are to complete a large project or stage a performance with many roles, then set up and prepare a larger group accordingly. If, on the other hand, you want to use a whole-class discussion, you must consider how to ensure that everyone benefits from it. Try whichever of the following formations best suits your instructional goals and students' learning needs:

- **Full-class:** Best for discussion that allows for maximum diversity of opinions. You can also use a seminar format or report out from smaller groups.

- **Large group:** Best for discussing an idea or text using a technique like literature circles. Such groups might have 5–8 students working on a project or performance.

- **Small group:** This configuration typically has 3–4 students who can serve as a quickly arranged group to discuss, construct, perform, or investigate.

- **Pairs:** Best for quick, responsive, even improvised, conversation. Use it when you feel students will benefit from checking with a classmate to compare ideas, problem-solving approaches, or solutions.

Model and teach the appropriate behaviors and skills for successful group work.

Like any behavior, working in groups or participating in a full-class activity requires modeling so that students can see what a successful performance looks like. This might mean demonstrating for the whole class or sitting down with a small group to show them how they should be discussing a text or working on a task. Here are some other approaches:

- Demonstrate how to participate in an academic discussion as part of the whole class or a smaller group. To do this I will pull together a group of students and use them to model how to discuss a text in a certain way.

- Identify and explain the specific behaviors appropriate to the activity, showing, for example, how a given role should be acted out in a lab, literature circle, or simulation.

- Have students who know what to do role play or otherwise illustrate the behavior for the class or group.

- Videotape effective groups and use the video to show groups in your current or future classes how to conduct themselves in the activity.

Keep in Mind Make sure that groups are culturally diverse but also appropriately balanced in light of potential cultural conflicts or objections.

Make effective transitions and maintain momentum during group instruction.

Movement from one activity to another is essential in any successful class. Throughout a typical period, three or four transitions occur that you must anticipate and prepare for to insure that the class sustains its momentum and students succeed. You can do several things to provide these transitions and maintain momentum when students work in groups:

- Write on the board the steps in the process that students will follow so they know what to expect and can prepare ahead of time for the sequence.

- Circulate among the groups to encourage them and maintain their momentum.

- Alert students to time limits or other transition points, signaling their approach and reminding them what they need to accomplish before that time.

- Explain why they are transitioning from one activity to another to clarify their purpose and your expectations.

- Structure the activity to culminate in a final activity that challenges students to work hard and well through the stages in preparation for that moment when they must present, perform, discuss, or write.

Monitor and provide feedback on group and individual performance.

Regardless of the configuration you use, it is essential that you monitor such factors as engagement, pace, comprehension, focus, and, of course, behavior. Without such a cycle of feedback and monitoring, students will do less work and do it less well. As the teacher, you must not only monitor students' progress but provide feedback that will help them be more insightful and efficient while working to meet the academic standards. To accomplish this, try the following:

- Pay attention to students' responses, using what they say and how they act to measure their understanding and focus.

- Circulate around the classroom when students are working in groups.

- Monitor the performance of English Learners, Special Education students, and others with special needs (including GATE) to keep them focused and challenged.

- Provide feedback to individuals or groups based on your observations of their work.

- Use a rubric to keep a record of who participates and how well; offer individuals, groups, or the whole class feedback based on this rubric so they know what they should be doing and how they can improve.

- Have students reflect on individual and group performance and processes—and how to improve them.

Learning for All

1. Meet the Needs of All Students

No one misbehaves when they are absorbed in what they are doing. That's why the best classroom management technique is one that meets students' desire to learn what they want to learn, especially the things they need to learn in order to achieve success in life. Many disruptions stem from boredom, frustration, or some combination of both. As Plato said, "Do not train boys to learn by force and harshness, but lead them by what amuses them, so they may better discover the best of their minds." What kids need is an education, a classroom that honors the spirit of the Greek Muses, the nine daughters of Zeus who presided over the arts and sciences. Instead of Greek goddesses, however, I offer a more contemporary muse in the form of instruction, based on sound research, that is *meaningful, useful, social,* and *engaging.* These four concepts are further developed in the principles that follow.

Guiding Principles

1. Instruction works best as guided inquiry into meaningful topics.

2. Lessons include the knowledge and skills students need to solve a range of academic and real-world problems.

3. Whenever appropriate, have students work with others to promote the social nature of learning.

4. What students learn and how they learn it engages the full range of their intelligence and abilities.

Instruction works best as guided inquiry into meaningful topics.

When students have some say in what they learn or how they learn it, they engage more fully in what the class is doing. In English that might mean providing students with a list of topics to choose from while reading a novel. Students interested in power, for example, can look for ideas and events related to that subject, while other students might prefer to read for ethics, relationships, or technology, taking notes as they read on what actually interests them. Your social studies class may be learning about Latin America, but you can give students choices about which aspect of that country to study by letting them study its PERSIA: *politics, economics, religion, society,* or *intellectual/artistic*

traditions. Inquiry, because it leads to increased engagement, results in better comprehension and retention—and fewer disruptions. Try the following to incorporate inquiry into your classroom instruction:

Maria Lilja

- Give students choices about their inquiry whenever possible, whether on papers, projects, or investigations.

- Ask the students what they know about or what experiences they have with this subject.

- Connect what students are studying to their knowledge and experience, to other texts and lessons, and to the world at large.

- Generate topics and essential questions with students to find out what interests them about the subject they are studying.

- Allow students to revise their guiding questions as the inquiry unfolds to make room for new discoveries about the subject or their own interests in the subject.

New Teacher Note! Serious inquiry—that is, productive, educational inquiry—is fundamentally different than the free-for-all "do your own thing" of the past. Inquiry-based instruction demands structure and teaches the skills and knowledge outlined by the standards in context. Inquiry, in other words, demands careful planning on your part if it is to be effective.

Lessons include the knowledge and skills students need to solve a range of academic and real-world problems.

Students want to know, as we all do, that what they learn will be of use. They are practical and, to the extent that they see how the lesson will help them do something they value, they will commit to the activity and thus work with—instead of against—you. You can address their concerns by trying the following:

- Identify and explain that you will teach them the skills and knowledge they need to succeed on this assignment.

- Connect what they are learning and doing in your class to other classes so they see that the skills and knowledge have a wider range of applications.

- Ask them how the skills and knowledge they are learning might apply to the world beyond school, adding your own examples after you hear theirs.

- Reinforce the different applications of skills throughout the activity when students are writing a paper or science report. For example in the fields of medicine or criminal justice, you must be able to draw conclusions from data and synthesize it in a report written for others.

- Build in reflection time that asks students to identify their strengths and challenges (areas they need to improve) and consider the skills they will need for success in the future.

Whenever appropriate, have students work with others to promote the social nature of learning.

Learning is inherently social. We learn from and for others. Today's workplace is more collaborative than ever, a reality that schools must address. We must teach students the skills needed to work with others to solve problems. This does not mean, however, that we should let them work together at all times. Try this:

- Assign the same task or activity to two groups, challenging them to come up with alternative solutions to the same problem. You'll find it will build excitement and curiosity.

- Organize the class into pairs or groups for focused, purposeful discussions about questions they generate or that the entire class is trying to answer.

- Arrange the class into groups (assigning or letting students choose specific roles based on their individual strengths) to work on a project or read a common text, then present what they learned to the class. In my English class, for example, I sometimes provide students with a list of topics designed to interest different students, who can then choose the one that interests them most.

- Consider ways to increase social interaction through the structured use of technology (e.g., online threaded discussions as a variation on literature circles). Returning to the previous example, once students choose their topic and form their groups, they must then contribute to online discussion about their topic, allowing students from different classes to contribute to the same conversation.

What students learn and how they learn it engages the full range of their intelligence and abilities.

School too often honors and focuses on narrowly conceived ideas of intelligence. Howard Gardner's work *The Disciplined Mind: What All Students Should Understand* challenges teachers to recognize and help students learn about their own multiple intelligences, which he identifies as *linguistic, logical-mathematical, musical, bodily-kinesthetic, spatial, interpersonal, intrapersonal,* and *naturalist.* To this list he has attached what he calls "existential intelligence," which refers to those introspective abilities one uses when grappling with the big questions that engage clerics, philosophers, and artists. Try the following when planning instruction:

- Incorporate multiple entry points into the curriculum from which students can choose: numerical, aesthetic, narrative, philosophical, physical, or social.

- Give the students choices about how they want to present the results of their inquiry (e.g., paper, presentation, project, model, or something else).

- Ask students to consider the same subject from multiple perspectives and then present what they learned in different—written, spoken, visual, dramatic, or musical—ways.

- Provide time and room for students to explore and create within the context of the assignment so they can get into the "flow" of their work and increase the likelihood of getting totally engaged in the problems the assignment presents.

2. Meet the Needs of English Language Learners

Currently, 9.9 million students (K–12) speak a language other than English at home, up from 3.8 million in 1979. While ethnicity does not necessarily mean one speaks a language other than English, the same U.S. Department of Education survey reports that between 1972 and 2004 the percentage of racial or ethnic minorities enrolled in public schools increased from 22 to 43 percent, with Hispanic students accounting for 19 percent of public school enrollment, a 6 percent increase since 1972. No one has to tell you that your classes have become more culturally, ethnically, and linguistically diverse: the evidence is arranged in front of you. While these students' primary educational needs are the same as all other students'—to learn what helps them succeed in school and beyond—English Learners have other needs specific to their circumstances. If you can meet those needs, you will help that student find a place not only in the classroom but in the school and society at large. While not the primary focus of this section, "cultural intelligence" has, in recent years, emerged as an essential set of skills for teachers, leaders, and business people working in the global economy. Thus English Learners offer native-speaking students important opportunities to learn about and prepare for the world.

Guiding Principles

1. Create a classroom climate that emphasizes being polite and respectful to everyone.

2. Provide clear, simple directions regarding behaviors and tasks.

3. Integrate English Language Learners into the class community.

4. Involve student, parents, and school faculty in helping ELLs.

5. Celebrate, don't ignore, cultural differences.

Create a classroom climate that emphasizes being polite and respectful to everyone.

Any time you have a room filled with 30 or more people from different places and backgrounds, there is potential for misunderstanding or even conflict. People bring their opinions, values, and experiences with them, some of which might be based on cultural biases, stereotypes, or assumptions. Thus it falls to you to help your students learn to work with everyone in the class, even if they have some prejudice toward or have experienced a past conflict with people from that ethnic group or country. Consider the following ideas for creating such a climate of politeness and respect:

- State clearly and immediately at the beginning of the year that you expect students to be polite to and show respect for each other.

- Model and define for students what it looks like to be considerate in different situations so students know what to say and do.

- Post a sign with examples of commonly used appropriate and inappropriate remarks and behaviors; add to it as situations arise, using it to remind and reinforce.

- Connect this value regularly to the adult workplace, emphasizing how important it is to work well with people from different backgrounds, cultures, and countries.

- Practice what you preach, being at all times a role model in these areas to all students.

Provide clear, simple directions regarding behaviors and tasks.

Students who do not know what to do are more likely to distract or disrupt the class. While good directions are important to all students, English Learners may not know what the words you use mean and may require additional clarity or explanation at times. Many classroom customs may be new or completely foreign to some students, some of whom may not have been in a classroom for some time, even years in some cases. Consider these strategies:

- Write directions on the board or overhead in clear language, arranged in numbered steps, in the same place every day, in different colors for different classes.

- Post a sign with the steps for common procedures for easy reference by all.

- Check with English Learners to be sure they understand the directions.

- Do not speak too fast.

- Demonstrate what to do as you explain how and why to do it.

- Ask other students who speak the same language to explain to those who don't understand what to do.

Integrate English Language Learners into the class community.

As with any new student, English Learners need to feel part of the classroom so they will thrive academically and also learn how to live within the American culture of which they are now a part. This integration should serve educational ends, such as learning to work with others across language and culture, and also serve personal ends, like developing their confidence through widening their social circle. Here are some suggested techniques:

- Assign English Learners to different groups instead of segregating them in their own; rotate the groups over time so they work with many different students.

- Give English Learners a designated role in groups and explain what to do, asking the group to provide additional guidance and support throughout the activity.

- Seat English Learners throughout the room—though toward the front—so they can better see and hear what you are saying.

- Anticipate and avoid situations that might embarrass or humiliate English Learners.

- Invite English Learners to make and share connections between your curriculum and their home country.

> **Legal Note** One issue that arises with some English Learners is their legal status in the country. It is not necessary or appropriate for teachers to inquire about this. If required to find out, seek legal advice as to whether you must comply with such a directive.

Involve student, parents, and school faculty in helping ELLs.

English Learners have a network of advocates and interested persons at school and home to help teachers. While language is sometimes a barrier, make use of this network at home as well as school to help your students get the services and support they need. Try the following if questions or problems arise:

- Begin by talking with students about their needs or any problems in the class.

- Consult with the ESL teacher or department about your students and any possible cultural or language issues.

- Consider meeting with students and their parents if your concerns cannot be resolved by conferring with the ESL teacher or the student.

- Ask the school nurse for vision and hearing tests if you suspect that undiagnosed problems might account for certain problems in class.

- Confer with the counselors or ESL teachers if you suspect possible cognitive, emotional, or behavioral differences might exist, so the student can be tested.

Celebrate, don't ignore, cultural differences.

Many schools have students walking the halls who, among them, speak over 100 languages. Along with those many languages comes a world of experiences and perspectives that stand to enrich your discussion of ideas, literature, government, and history if you make room for them in your classes. Here are some ideas for incorporating cultural diversity in your classroom:

Maria Lilja

- Invite students to make their own cultural connections when doing an art project, researching history, or reading books of their own choice for English.

- Provide opportunities for all students to investigate some aspect of their culture and bring it into the classroom to share with all.

- Ensure that all cultures feel equally honored and included.

- Acknowledge, address, and resolve cultural conflicts that arise in the classroom instead of pretending they do not exist.

- Transcend individual culture and language by creating your own classroom culture that honors what students do and think more than where they are from or what language they speak.

3. Support Students With Special Needs

Approximately 25 percent of the students at any school have special needs. These needs fall along a continuum of intensity, but they all have the potential to affect students' performance and the class as a whole. Some students struggle to control both behavior and mind as they grapple with such conditions as ADD/ADHD. Some students have mental disorders that manifest themselves in self-destructive behaviors such as cutting or eating disorders; others suffer debilitating periods such as depression, manic states, or anxiety attacks. To these challenges, we must add various processing disorders (visual, auditory, linguistic) and sensorimotor problems. Finally, certain trends, such as the dramatic rise in the number of children born with autism, suggest new and continued challenges for teachers such as yourself who walk into the classroom expecting simply to teach only the subject you were hired to teach. You do not get to choose your students; what you can choose are the methods you use to help all students—and thus yourself—succeed.

Guiding Principles

1. Know that all students, despite their special needs, can benefit from, contribute to, and succeed in your class.

2. Communicate effectively with the student, parents, and members of that student's support network.

3. Develop your students' independence and their ability to advocate for what they need.

4. Use a variety of instructional solutions to meet each student's individual needs.

5. Create a classroom environment that is sensitive to special-needs students.

Know that all students, despite their special needs, can benefit from, contribute to, and succeed in your class.

Attitude is everything. Students who walk into a class and find a teacher who is supportive will work for that teacher. Your students respond to you if you meet them where they are and are willing to help them get where they need to be. Students with special needs want more than just empathy and commitment; they want respect for what they know and bring to the class. To accomplish these ends, you need to:

- Establish a relationship with each student that shows you care and are committed to helping her succeed in your class.

- Ask the student, if you are unsure, what he needs to be able to succeed on a given assignment or task.

- Include questions that provide for a range of responses, all of which would be valid and meaningful.

- Reflect on how you are speaking to, responding to, evaluating, or including students with special needs and consider how you might better show your commitment to or appreciation of them and what they bring to the class.

- Consult the student's parents and support specialists (e.g., psychologist, resource teacher, assigned aide) to learn how else you might provide opportunities for that student to shine or otherwise benefit from your class.

Legal Note! Know everything you can about students' Individual Education Programs (IEPs), especially the prescribed accommodations or suggested modifications. If unclear about anything related to a student's IEP consult the special education department.

Communicate effectively with the student, parents, and members of that student's support network.

Communication is essential to any student's success but especially the student with special needs. First, you need to know what those needs are. And then, you must learn from others how you can best meet them. As the year progresses, you may want to communicate information about the student's success or concerns about the student's lack of success. Parents and other members of the student's support team will likely communicate with you, sometimes with great urgency or frequency. You need to find ways to communicate with the student and others who help the student succeed without taking too much of the time you should be spending preparing to be an effective teacher. Try the following:

- Meet with the student to get to know him and find out what he needs to succeed, especially when it comes to communicating directions or choosing instructional strategies (e.g., working in groups).

- Write legibly in clear, concise language, using (if helpful) different colors or other such strategies to help special needs students process and understand information.

- Arrange some private means of communicating (e.g., a signal) between the two of you, so that the student can discreetly let you know she needs help or permission to step out for a minute to relax or go to the special education teacher for support.

- Provide the special education teacher, aide, and parents (by e-mail for efficiency if possible) with assignments and related information in advance so they can provide extra support up front to ensure the student's success.

- Communicate concerns about students you think might have potential learning and behavior problems to the appropriate counselors or other faculty at your school so they can initiate the necessary evaluations. Include examples or evidence if possible, as well as strategies you've tried, to help them determine the nature of the student's problems.

Index Open

Develop your students' independence and their ability to advocate for what they need.

One of the fundamental principles of special needs education is that students should be placed in the "least restrictive environment." Central to this tenet is the idea that students must develop independence as a means to living as the adults they will eventually become. Another key aspect of inclusive education is self-advocacy, which means teaching students to advocate for what they need to succeed. You can help your students develop these abilities by doing the following:

- Have on hand a copy of the recommended or required accommodations for each student in class and meet with those students and, if necessary, their support team to come up with strategies for implementing those accommodations effectively but independently.

- Do not over help. Do not do for students what they can do themselves.

- Ask students ahead of time what they will need to succeed on an assignment, providing a helpful and obvious opportunity for the student to ask for the extra time on the test, for example, that his IEP allows.

- Provide students structured choices that will lead to success; making choices is important to all students as a means of charting their own course of success.

- Monitor students' progress and have them identify, during and after an assignment, which strategies or actions helped them complete the assignment.

New Teacher Note! Create codes for your seating chart that can serve as a shorthand to remind you of students' different needs and required accommodations.

Use a variety of instructional solutions to meet each student's individual needs.

Special education instructional solutions fall into two categories: *accommodations* and *modifications*. Some methods, such as differentiated instruction, span the two, providing a broad practical framework for meeting students' needs and building on their strengths. Accommodations typically mean allowing students to complete the same assignment or test but with allowances for time and environment. On tests, for example, students get more time or are allowed to work in a separate environment more conducive to their learning. Differentiated instruction encourages teachers to "differentiate" the product, the process, or the content itself. You can provide such support to your special needs students by trying the following:

- Allow these students more time on assignments or tests, perhaps working with an aide in a different, quieter room.

- Format assignments, presentations, or even the whiteboard in different ways (e.g., using color or boxes) to help them process information more effectively.

- Permit students to demonstrate their understanding of the material by some other means (e.g., student-teacher conference, presentations, visual representation).

- Suggest the student read a different (e.g., shorter, easier) book on the same subject so he can participate but at a more suitable level.

- Let the student complete a portion of an assignment to show she understands the basic principles but hold all others to the higher standard and require they complete the whole assignment.

- Ask special education teachers to help adapt or create alternative tests that represent the integrity of the content while addressing the students' instructional needs.

Create a classroom environment that is sensitive to special needs students.

Some special needs students need to sit in designated places such as the front (as indicated by their IEP). Others, perhaps owing to wheelchairs or other physical supports, require dedicated spaces. Many, of course, just walk in and sit down wherever they want and get to work. Still, others will be distracted or somehow undermined by certain environmental factors. The following suggestions will help you provide a productive learning environment for all students:

- Ask students to evaluate the room for potential distractions or obstacles so you can remove them and show you are committed to their success and safety.

- Seat students with special needs according to their IEP or, if no such information is available, wherever seems most appropriate to their needs.

- Provide duplicates so students with physical limitations do not have to carry books home.

- Provide alternative stations where special needs students can work with an aide or use the computer to do their work (as may be required by their IEPs).

- Be consistent in your use of words, whiteboards, and resources in the class so students know what to expect and how the class works.

4. Support Students With Specific Learning Disabilities

In recent years, teachers find many more students with ADD/ADHD and autism entering their classes. In short, students with "learning disabilities" have difficulty taking in, attending to, retrieving, processing, understanding, or expressing ideas and information, and this is most often manifested in difficulties with reading, calculating, spelling, writing, understanding or expressing language, coordination, self-control, or social skills. This chapter, while focused on instruction, looks at what we teachers can do to help these students succeed in their classes—and ensure a safe, productive environment.

Guiding Principles

- Students who suffer from attention disorders need a structured, distraction-free environment.

- Students with visual processing disorders need help understanding and using visual information.

- Students with auditory processing disorders need additional support understanding what is said and what to do.

- Students with sensorimotor difficulties need help both understanding and executing directions and actions.

- Students with behavioral disorders need clear guidelines and consistent enforcement.

Students who suffer from attention disorders need a structured, distraction-free environment.

Stimuli outside and within these students—noises, movements, thoughts, colors or patterns—make it difficult for them to pay attention to or understand what they see or hear. While they may appear inattentive to others—and often are—they also have exceptional abilities to immerse themselves in activities or information they enjoy. Try the following:

- Create a positive environment with predictable structure.

- Provide clear guidelines and concise directions for behavior and activities.

- Assign the student a seat near you, preferably in the front to reduce distractions.

- Provide written directions broken down into steps they can check off; go through the directions orally as well, demonstrating what they are to do.

- Redirect their attention, offer them choices, and focus on their strengths.

- Use proximity and agreed upon cues known only to the particular students to help students focus.

Image Source/Getty Images

Students with visual processing disorders need help understanding and using visual information.

Information presented visually—on a whiteboard, through a video, via LCD projector, or simply on paper—is difficult for these students to understand, often requiring an effort that exhausts them. Though they have no actual sight impairment, they can have difficulty discriminating visual information. Lacking an awareness of physical distance, these students can sometimes struggle with social relationships or understanding spatial relationships. Here are some ways you can assist such students in your class:

- Ask these students what helps them best process information; use their responses to develop strategies that will improve their performance.

- Present information orally as well as visually so they can hear what they are seeing and process it using another, perhaps stronger, faculty.

Maria Lilja

- Use special features—color coding, arranging information spatially, adding organizational structures such as numbering—when preparing materials.

- Consider, in some cases, providing an alternative means for them to complete the assignment and demonstrate their learning.

- Check with these students at the beginning of labs, projects, or other activities to assess their readiness and ask what accommodations they need to succeed.

Students with auditory processing disorders need additional support understanding what is said and what to do.

For these students, information gets in but often gets confused or misunderstood. These students will have a hard time following verbal directions or doing such things as taking notes from a lecture or video. When attempting such activities, these students often need more time. Without it, they can become frustrated and feel exhausted. Try these ideas to support these students:

- Provide, whenever possible, written directions, notes, and outlines so the student can focus on the content rather than struggling to take notes.

- Demonstrate or provide examples of what a successful performance looks like so the student can see what must be done.

- Use the whiteboard to capture ideas and information during a discussion.

- Organize information using colors and spatial arrangements to help these students better process content, especially as it relates to a series of actions they must follow or remember.

- Allow the students extra time when they must take notes from a lecture or a video or complete assignments that require them to listen and write.

Students with sensorimotor difficulties need help both understanding and executing directions and actions.

When processing information, these students often experience a miscue of the brain which affects their language, coordination, spatial skills, memory, and behavioral inhibition. Often these students struggle to combine sensory input (fine or gross motor, spatial body awareness) to complete classroom activities or academic tasks, typically leading them to experience such activities as frustrating and potentially humiliating. Help these students by providing a range of accommodations such as:

- Allow them to use "buddy notes" (i.e., copy the notes of a successful classmate who takes excellent, legible notes).

- Allow the use of a scribe (someone hired or provided to take notes).

- Suggest technological adaptations and supports such as Kurzweil readers or audio books.

- Consult and collaborate with the student's assigned aide or occupational therapist.

Arthur Tilley/Taxi/Getty Images

Students with behavioral disorders need clear guidelines and consistent enforcement.

As teachers see increasing numbers of students with Asperger's Syndrome and other forms of autism, you can expect students who lack the social skills needed to work with others or function comfortably in a large heterogeneous class. These students, while often extremely intelligent when it comes to learning and remembering facts, struggle to understand the information or use it to solve problems or apply it to other situations. In addition, they quickly become agitated or confused when a situation lacks predictable structure. Despite these difficulties, they are often capable of succeeding in general education classes, though their behavior may in some instances invite ridicule or teasing from their peers. Consider these ideas when working with such students:

- Keep instructions brief and clear. If possible, provide the directions in writing (on paper or the board) or, as an alternative, just give them a few steps at a time.

- Provide visual models or demonstrations as these students learn visually, but avoid combining visual and oral information simultaneously because they have trouble processing information in this dual form.

- Anticipate and prevent anxiety-causing incidents by preparing the students (often through a short narrative about what they will do in class that day) for an upcoming experience that may be new to them.

- Allow them to use their strengths—computers, drawing, interest in a particular topic—whenever possible to ensure their success on an assignment.

- Work with the student's special education teacher to prepare for upcoming activities, experiences, or assignments that might pose problems for the student.

Positive Discipline

1. Teach Self-Discipline and Personal Responsibility

So far I've focused on what you can do to manage your students effectively. Yet it is the students who must ultimately be able to manage themselves in order to succeed in school, the workplace, and their lives outside of institutional settings. Such personal responsibility for their own behavior begins with students knowing themselves well; they must also, however, develop some awareness of what measures help them focus, behave, and work well and appropriately. Researchers refer to this set of skills and factors as "emotional or social intelligence," which they define as those personal management and social skills that allow a person to succeed in work and in life outside of work. Within this definition, scholars include such essential skills as being aware of one's own needs in a situation and how to best meet those needs to achieve success.

Guiding Principles

1. Develop students' awareness of what is appropriate in a given situation.

2. Teach students to monitor their actions, attitudes, and needs.

3. Help students identify and use strategies to manage themselves.

4. Evaluate the effectiveness of these strategies.

5. Revise or develop new strategies to improve self-discipline.

Develop students' awareness of what is appropriate in a given situation.

Personal discipline for students begins with knowledge of what they must do, then training themselves to do it despite their inclination not to. For many students, school is like a country whose culture and conventions they must learn, especially in classrooms where the demands are high and the behaviors can seem foreign. Such high demands on us as teachers complicate our work; we already lack the time needed to teach all we're expected to in the course of a semester. So where do we find the time, and how do we even begin, to teach students how to manage themselves? We can begin by trying the following:

- Post on the wall or write on the board what is appropriate before students engage in the activity, go on the excursion, meet the guest speaker, or use the lab.

- Have students generate the traits of effective participation in activities like these listed above, and explain how they contribute to their success in that situation.

- Create a list of what is not appropriate in the classroom and discuss why it is not.

Image Source/Getty Images

- Discuss what behavior is appropriate to a specific situation, especially one with which students have little or no prior experience.

New Teacher Note! You set the standard for behavior and attitude in all situations. Share what you do to keep yourself in line; for example, you might tell your students the self-management strategies you used during the incredibly boring school presentation on railway safety.

Teach students to monitor their actions, attitudes, and needs.

Self-control is at the heart of individual success, yet people cannot control themselves if they are not aware of their mental and emotional conditions. These thoughts and feelings influence how people act and what they believe in a given situation. Thus students' ability to adjust their behavior or emotions depends on developing the capacity to monitor these conditions, just as they might monitor the instrument panel in the car while driving. You can teach students to monitor themselves by trying the following:

- Identify those areas they should monitor: physical and emotional reactions, verbal responses, attitudes and intentions, physical and emotional needs.

- Have students generate a list of their reactions and needs, such as interrupting, tapping their feet, drumming on desktops, judging, or talking.

- Ask them to write about the when, how, and why of these different actions and reactions, and what effect they have on their performance or attitude.

- Provide some form of feedback to help them see themselves: a seating chart with tally marks for certain behaviors or even a video clip showing them how they behave.

- Require students to list all that they did during the course of a day and evaluate each activity according to whether it gave them energy (GE) or took energy (TE), then analyze the results, focusing on what takes energy and how they can address that.

Help students identify and use strategies to manage themselves.

Now that they have reflected on their individual needs and reactions, students must determine how to use that awareness to improve their behavior and performance. Each student needs to find those strategies that work best for her. The following techniques are a good way to begin that process:

- Work with individual students to create a cue word or some reminder they can use when they notice they are about to behave, think, or feel in a way that is counterproductive.

- Set up some system students can use to remind themselves what to watch for or what to do. This might include a note on their desk to look at a checklist or poster periodically to help them focus on and monitor their behavior.

- Develop and use a language of responsibility that teaches students to attribute their successes and mistakes to themselves not to teachers, classmates, or the situation.

- Consult with parents, counselors, or other teachers to find strategies that work, and then help the students use those in your class.

Keep in Mind In some cases a behavior you see as a problem may be entirely appropriate in the culture from which a student comes. Seek first to understand the behavior, emotional reaction, or attitude in the context of that student's culture before explaining how people in the United States might view this or respond.

Evaluate the effectiveness of these strategies.

Teachers and students must continually evaluate the effect of any strategy students try. There are several aspects to such an evaluation, including how your students feel about the technique, and how the technique makes your students feel. Despite being somewhat awkward, the technique might nonetheless work and thus give students an increased feeling of self-control. Try one of the following methods of evaluating the strategies you and your students are using.

- Keep a tally on your seating chart or use a sticky note tracking the number of times the student engages in a certain behavior.

- Add these tally scores to a graph or table that shows whether the technique is working.

- Create a troubleshooting poster or page for individuals or the class with a column that identifies problems (if x) and solutions (then y).

- Discuss with the student, or have her write about, why a strategy is working; if it is not working, meet to discuss why it is not and what might work better.

- Ask the student to reflect in writing at the end of an activity, a designated period of time, the class period, or the school day on his behavior and performance and the effect of the intervention in these areas.

- Videotape and review with the student her behavior during a specified time or activity to help that student see and better understand the behavior.

Revise or develop new strategies to improve self-discipline.

After reflecting on the results of whatever strategies have been used or changes have been made, you need to use that information to improve—or replace—the method. Consider using one of these recommendations:

Image Source/Corbis

- Ask the student first what can be improved and how; then work with the student to implement those changes.

- Make incremental changes in order to determine what does and does not work, what is and is not part of the problem, instead of making sudden, sweeping changes that might mask what makes the real difference.

- Focus on strengths and what is working, building on what works and what the student does best.

- Help the student analyze why this new technique should work better by discussing it, modeling it, or role-playing it.

2. Administer Discipline With Dignity

Standing in the middle of a large classroom surrounded by equipment and supplies, you can feel a bit like the head of an emergency room: You have to monitor everything that is going on simultaneously, doing triage to determine whose needs are most important, and preventing any deterioration in the condition of the people for whom that ER team leader is responsible. To all that, add potential cultural, personal, and interpersonal issues, all of which can season the class with extra tension (and rich opportunities for teaching). In the midst of this swirl of energy called a classroom, you must not only work but lead, guiding the team toward the chosen destination with a combination of discipline and dignity. As George Washington, speaking about his unruly and unprepared troops in the American Revolution, said: "We get the men we do and must shape them into the people we need them to be."

Guiding Principles

1. Attend to all details regarding behavior, movement, and interaction.

2. Respond quickly and effectively to students' behaviors before trouble begins.

3. Address students in an objective tone regarding behavior and attitude.

4. Be equitable in all disciplinary matters.

4. Show students respect at all times, even when you discipline them.

Attend to all details regarding behavior, movement, and interaction.

Something is always happening—or about to happen—in any classroom where a large, diverse group of students gathers. It might not be a fight but could be, instead, a conflict that stems from an ancient grudge going back to fourth grade, tension based on cultural conflict, or a thoughtless word uttered to the wrong person on the wrong day. Other conditions for which you must develop an ear and eye include students upset by personal problems, drugs, or issues in the larger school environment that might be upsetting them. Improve awareness by focusing on these initial steps:

- Maintain visual contact with the class and each student throughout the period. If you must talk to a student or someone entering your class, do not turn your back to the class.

- Move around the room during the class to monitor what students are doing and show that you are attentive to their every move.

- Know who is likely to try to do work for other classes, cause trouble, or otherwise be off-task and keep an extra eye on those students.

- Monitor students' state as they enter, paying close attention for signs of distress, depression, anger, or intoxication.

- Listen and watch for any tension that might begin to arise between students or from individuals in response to topics, activities, or proximity.

AbleStock/Index Open

New Teacher Note! Many teachers find it difficult to confront students with confidence and calm. Try rehearsing or visualizing how you will confront students in a difficult situation in the future. Also, ask more experienced colleagues how they would handle a similar situation.

Respond quickly and effectively to students' behaviors before trouble begins.

The more adept you become at monitoring the room and your students' behavior, the more you will be able to spot and prevent potential trouble. Students who think, "Man, that teacher sees everything! You can't get away with anything! She's got eyes in the back of her head!" don't try to get away with anything; just your presence alone helps to maintain order and discipline. The attentive, responsive teacher quickly identifies the problem and its source, then moves decisively to intervene in a calm, professional manner. Here are a few things to consider for your classroom:

- Call a particular student aside for a quiet discussion about his behavior or condition.

- Avoid publicly humiliating a student as this can escalate a situation.

- Write a quick note to a student who seems distressed or otherwise upset, asking what is wrong and how you can help.

- Use humor to ease the tension within the class or between students.

- Offer choices, when appropriate, but reinforce your role as the one in charge.

Address students in an objective tone regarding behavior and attitude.

While not always easy to do, you'll accomplish much more by not getting emotionally involved in a situation with students. This is not to say that you should be cold and distant, or that you should talk like an overly officious mall security guard; instead, maintaining sufficient objectivity allows you to act impartially, thereby defusing the situation and reinforcing your credibility as the adult in the situation. Here are some tips to maintaining an objective tone:

- Do not personalize your actions or remarks when confronting a student.

- Strike a nonchalant, easy-going manner to avoid escalating the tension.

- Leave adequate room between you and the student to reduce tension.

- Focus on observable behaviors so the subject of the discussion is the behavior or attitude, not the student— or you.

- Avoid using a sarcastic, ironic, or judgmental tone that might undermine your effectiveness.

Keep in Mind Cultural conflict—whether it stems from racism, stereotypes, or historical antipathy in their native countries—is a common source of trouble in class. Find out the source of any tension and, while working to resolve it, consider it when designing assignments, choosing partners, or assigning seats.

Be equitable in all disciplinary matters.

Students, especially adolescents, are sensitive to any slight or injustice they might suffer at the hands of adults. Of course, what they claim is "no fair!" adults are likely to see as appropriate and just. While we teachers should never steer by students' ethical compass when tending to discipline, we must be mindful that we apply our policies consistently to all. Consider the following when striving for this difficult objective:

- Give no appearance of preferential treatment when it comes to disciplinary action.

- Do not make exceptions for some and not for others when addressing problems, especially based on gender, race, or academic standing.

- Direct serious infractions to the administration so that major consequences can come from those who are more objective.

- Apply the same level of consequence (e.g., phone call to parents, referral to administration, meeting with school safety advocate) to all.

- Maintain emotional objectivity to reinforce consistency and equity instead of showing sympathy to some but not all.

Show students respect at all times, even when you discipline them.

No question about it: it can be difficult for a person to respect someone who is not showing mutual respect. Still, it is important for us as teachers to remember that we are teaching students, shaping them, helping them learn not only the lessons of the subject but also those of life. Sometimes we expect students to be what they are not yet ready to be: mature, reasoning adults who think before they act. The following suggestions offer some initial guidance in how to treat students you must discipline:

- Ask whenever possible why the students are behaving as they are, as sometimes the behavior is a manifestation of some deeper trouble that also needs attention.

- Avoid the dance that brings you down to the level of the student until you are acting like the 14-year-old you are trying to govern.

- Provide students with choices, if possible, since those who are trapped and feel their dignity threatened will do anything to prevent being humiliated.

- Follow the Golden Rule, doing nothing to that student that you would not want done or said to you (or your own child).

- See each disciplinary situation as an opportunity to teach instead of a chance to crush, shame, or otherwise degrade a student.

3. Communicate Policies, Procedures, and Principles in Your Syllabus

Along with your classroom, your policies, procedures, and principles define you early on, especially if spelled out in the syllabus on the first day. If you offer no rules or guidance in how to act or work in class, students have no reason to expect an organized, productive classroom. What's more, these policies and procedures can, in some cases, have legal ramifications or be linked to your performance evaluation and thus determine whether you are asked back or granted tenure.

Guiding Principles

1. Use a course syllabus to define and explain your policies and procedures.

2. Include details about required materials, course texts, and other relevant information.

3. Articulate your professional and instructional philosophy to both students and parents.

4. Ensure that your classroom policies and procedures comply with all local and federal regulations.

5. Review your syllabus for clarity, correctness, and content.

REGULAR SCHEDULE		1-HR. LATE START	
1°	8:00 – 8:51	1°	9:00 – 9:42
2°	8:56 – 9:52	2°	9:47 – 10:34
Passing Break	9:52 – 9:57	Passing Break	10:34 – 10:39
3°	10:02 – 10:53	3°	10:44 – 11:26
4°	10:58 – 11:49	4°	11:31 – 12:13
Lunch	11:49 – 12:19	Lunch	12:13 – 12:46
5°	12:24 – 1:15	5°	12:51 – 1:33
6°	1:20 – 2:11	6°	1:38 – 2:20
7°	2:16 – 3:07	7°	2:25 – 3:07

BHS Counselors

A-E	MS. LATHAM
F-M	MS. ESRAILIAN
N-Z	MRS. BUCKLEY

Use a course syllabus to define and explain your policies and procedures.

Effective teachers establish academic and behavioral expectations early, which helps students understand how the class works; such boundaries allow students to feel comfortable and secure so they can focus on learning in and enjoying the class. Research suggests limiting policies to no more than five, each of which should be clearly worded, demonstrated, and applied consistently and fairly. Consider these suggestions:

- Discuss and clarify policies with students regarding attendance, homework, plagiarism, electronic devices, missing work, and hall passes.

- Demonstrate and reinforce policies, explaining reasons and consequences.

- Define consequences without making threats or using negative language.

- Assess students' understanding of the policies and procedures.

- Refine and reiterate expectations as each new semester begins.

- Post policies and procedures on the class wall and on your Web site for reference and review.

 New Teacher Note! Ask several different colleagues and, if you are new, administrators to review your syllabus before distributing it.

These days too many issues have potentially serious consequences (for us), so it is best to spell out your policies and the consequences for any of the following that apply to your class:

- Academic honesty/plagiarism
- Attendance
- Bathroom/hall pass
- Beginning and end of the period
- Challenging grades
- Checking out materials
- Computer use
- Dress code
- Electronic devices
- Extra credit
- Food and drinks
- Grades for group work
- Journals
- Lab equipment
- Late work
- Making up work/tests
- Necessary supplies
- Seating assignment
- Shop tools

Include details about required materials, course texts, and other relevant information.

In addition to outlining your class policies and procedures, you can use the syllabus to communicate important information about the course and materials students will need. Be cautious about requiring students to buy materials, such as books, which the school is legally bound to provide. Some items in the following list, such as the course contract, are more common, for example, in AP classes where teachers want to be sure the student and parents understand and accept the demands of the course before it's too late. Consider including these common elements:

- Assigned textbooks
- Contact information
- Course contract
- Course description
- Course objectives and standards
- Mission statement
- Office hours
- Required supplies

Articulate your professional and instructional philosophy to both students and parents.

Many effective teachers include, usually at the beginning of the year or semester, a statement about their teaching philosophy. This mission statement, as with businesses that follow the same practice, challenges you to publicly declare your responsibilities to both the students and the curriculum, as it does the following:

- Specifies what this course teaches students to know and be able to do.

- Defines the source of your expectations and standards.

- Establishes your commitment to and belief in all students and their potential to succeed and learn.

- Clarifies what matters most in this course and why.

- Demonstrates your passion for the subject and your ability to teach it.

Ensure that your classroom policies and procedures comply with local and federal regulations.

Schools are governed by restrictions and laws as never before, many of them specific to what we can teach and how. Schools that do not make steady gains can, in many cases, be legally "reconstituted." Teachers now must ensure that what they teach will prepare students for state exit exams and other such consequential exams. Thus your syllabus should stress the role of the standards and demonstrate your commitment to helping students achieve those standards. Include the following in your syllabus, if pertinent:

- Identify any exams (AP, exit exam, state assessments) students in your course will be required to take.

- State your commitment to helping all students pass these exams.
- Confirm that the curriculum of your course will prepare them to meet the required standards and pass the exams.

Review your syllabus for clarity, correctness, and content.

Every document we distribute to our students reflects on our professionalism. This is never more true than during those first few days when we are handing out the syllabus and the first assignments. Think about trying the following:

- Format the document in a professional manner that is easy to read but appealing.
- Proofread the document yourself in addition to using the spell checker on your computer.
- Review the content to make sure it is current.
- Collaborate with other teachers of the same class to make sure you are all aligned in content and purpose.
- Avoid using too many or wacky fonts on the syllabus as this is something of a legal document and should establish that you are a serious teacher.
- Require students and their parents to sign and date the syllabus at the bottom to show they read and understand what you expect.

4. Establish and Maintain an Effective Approach to Discipline

Students learn little if the classroom is out of control. A disruptive classroom can reduce actual instructional time by 50 percent or more, fragmenting the instructional narrative so badly that kids disengage or, worse, learn nothing. New teachers consistently cite classroom discipline as their primary concern, a logical but not inevitable consequence of being new. Some experienced teachers will offer the sage advice that one should "not smile until December," but that approach raises questions instead of providing answers. What kids want most is a classroom in which they feel safe and secure, one which is predictable and stable; they want to know someone is in control, that someone will set appropriate limits and enforce them consistently and fairly so they can learn to succeed.

Guiding Principles

1. Prevent discipline problems before they start.
2. Create an effective teacher persona based on a strong ethos.
3. Use discipline to provide students with feedback about their behavior.
4. Do not do what does not work.
5. Base your plan on the features of effective discipline.

Prevent discipline problems before they start.

Many behavior problems stem from boredom or the students' belief that they cannot succeed at a task. Instead of asking what you can do to *control* students' counterproductive behavior, you might ask why students engage in such behavior in the first place; you might find it hard to comply with some of the work you assign your students. Effective discipline programs begin with an effective curriculum and a classroom culture that make such behavior inappropriate in the eyes of the students themselves. You may be able to prevent discipline problems by doing the following:

- Communicate your discipline policies as soon as possible, including the criteria and consequences.

- Provide a meaningful, engaging curriculum for all your students that considers their strengths and addresses their weaknesses.

- Anticipate students' needs and provide the necessary instruction to insure their success on the assignment or in the activity.

- Create a sense of community in your class so students feel included and committed to the success of that community and its members.

- Develop a relationship with students as soon as possible that is compassionate and fair but firm.

New Teacher Note! Seek out experienced teachers for advice and support, especially those teachers whose teaching style you most respect and want to emulate. Bring specific examples to the conversation. Ask: "What would you do in such a situation or with such a student?"

Create an effective teacher persona based on a strong ethos.

Ethos refers to a combination of elements such as force of personality, knowledge, and integrity. You earn students' respect if you are fair and consistent but govern with compassion and respect. Students will respond to and perform for you if they respect you, even give you permission to push that student harder to meet those higher expectations. Students working hard to meet such expectations rarely have time or inclination to misbehave. You can create such a teacher persona if you are:

- Decisive and reflective, reinforcing your role by showing you are in command and are confident but also willing to revisit and revise policies and decisions when it is appropriate.

- Consistent and considerate in your enforcement and interpretation of your policies and rules.

- Clear and concise when communicating limits, consequences, expectations, and directions.

- Fair and flexible, showing appropriate consideration for students during times of distress or a commitment to hearing all sides of a story before deciding on the consequences.

- Authoritative but not authoritarian, conveying a strong professional integrity about what you know and do in the classroom without basing your actions on fear and coercion.

Use discipline to provide students with feedback about their behavior.

Discipline is simply a means of providing feedback to a student about his behavior. The goal, of course, is to increase the quality and frequency of appropriate behavior and decrease and, ultimately, eliminate inappropriate behaviors that undermine instruction and learning. Try the following methods for giving students feedback:

- Provide verbal feedback by praising or reminding, clarifying or correcting, encouraging or commanding, using such feedback to improve or maintain behavior.

- Consider physical means such as gesturing to redirect their actions, moving closer to the student(s), removing distracting objects to help them focus, or moving the student to a better location for completing the work.

- Use written comments (on papers, index cards, or e-mail) to the student and his or her parents to acknowledge productive behavior or address counterproductive behavior.

- Model for students what they should be doing so they know what appropriate behavior in this context looks like.

- Have students reflect on their behavior during an activity, identifying, for example, the traits of effective participation in a group discussion and using generic examples from the current activity to illustrate those points without singling out students.

Legal Note Know what the laws of your state and the policies of your school allow when it comes to discipline. What, for example, is the school's policy on cheating? Document any incidents or disciplinary actions for future reference.

Do not do what does not work.

The best rule to follow is this: Only do what makes a difference. Of course, it needs to be a sustainable difference. Anything works once; the question is whether it is an effective technique that you can use over time to maintain a productive learning community. This also means that you must routinely reflect on what you do and the difference it does or does not make. The problem with punishing students is that one student's punishment is another's reward: "Send me out of class? Thank you!" Consider the following suggestions and the difference they can make:

- Do not threaten students in personal or otherwise intimidating ways that might engender resentment and retribution instead of achieve discipline and improvement.

- Avoid issuing repeated warnings, which undermines cohesive instruction.

- Resist the urge to blame students for the failure of an activity.

- Reevaluate whether detention will make a difference, especially when it means you must be there to supervise it.
- Remove a student from the classroom for disruptive behavior.

Base your plan on the features of effective discipline.

While each class presents its own discipline challenges, researchers have identified certain features of effective discipline. Like the expert who learns to use the right tool for the job, teachers must learn which approach is best in a given context. Marzano (2003) identifies five responses as being the most effective:

- **Teacher reaction:** The teacher reacts along a continuum depending on whether the behavior is positive or negative, beginning with verbal responses before moving on to more decisive interventions such as gestures, standing near the student, or other actions outlined above.

- **Tangible recognition:** The teacher may reward students for behaving appropriately or ceasing counterproductive behaviors, giving or taking (e.g., points, tokens) based on clearly defined criteria.

- **Direct cost:** The teacher uses this approach only to eliminate negative behaviors, but such an approach requires consistency and clarity of purpose, otherwise students might question the teacher's integrity. Examples of this approach include losing the opportunity to do certain things (recess), use resources (computer), or go places (field trips).

- **Group contingency:** The teacher can reward the whole group for completing a task or, in a variation considered more risky, reward the group based on the performance of specific students in the group. This second approach runs the risk of humiliating the student who fails the group.

- **Home contingency:** The teacher can make an effective difference by communicating both praise and concern, especially when unexpected, to the student's parents. Such communication may be done by phone, e-mail, written note, or scheduled conference.

Troubleshooting

Now you have general classroom management down, but every day is something new. This section offers succinct summaries to those most common challenges we as teachers face in the classroom, challenges which may not have been specifically addressed in the previous sections of the book. It identifies the primary areas of the problem and lists actions you can use to prevent or resolve problems in that area. Think of it as a quick reference guide to turn to before troubles arises; in the event that a crisis is unfolding, turn here for immediate guidance. It is always a good idea, however, to seek out more experienced colleagues, counselors, and administrators to help you if anything occurs that could possibly endanger your students, the school, or your own standing as a respected professional.

1. Assignments

Problems to Watch For: Students who

- Do not do the assigned work at all
- Turn in work that is incomplete or not their own
- Submit work that is of poor quality
- Fail to turn in work that they actually do

If students consistently have trouble turning in, completing, or doing assignments:

1. Pose the most obvious question to them: *Why are you not doing the work?*

2. Evaluate who is actually doing the work at the level you expect.

Maria Lilja

3. Ask yourself: *Do students have a reason to do this work besides avoiding a zero? Is the work engaging and does it have inherent value—or is it "busywork?"*

4. Provide opportunities for collaboration on assignments as a way of providing help and getting the work done by everyone, especially those who need the assistance that collaboration provides.

5. Assess the time needed to do the assignment; keep in mind that students may not have help or resources at home and may have homework for several other classes.

6. Give them time to begin the work in class so they can confer with you for help; or designate time outside of class when they can come for extra help or a space in which to do the work.

7. Provide them with models of how to do the work so they go home knowing what a successful performance on this assignment looks like.

8. Explain the directions for the homework clearly, leaving time for questions about the parts of the assignment they do not understand.

9. Try giving less work (e.g., five instead of ten math problems, ten instead of twenty vocabulary words) to see if more students will actually complete it.

10. Be consistent: Students quickly develop expectations about what classes demand, so they learn that math has homework every night but that another class gives it every once in a while. In such a case, students often do not do the homework for the other class as it is not a part of their evening ritual the way the math homework is.

2. Attendance

Problems to Watch For:

- Excused absences for one or two days
- Excused absences for a prolonged period of time due to a family trip, college visits, serious illness, performances, or competitions
- Excused tardies due to school events, meetings with school officials, or staying after to finish a test or talk with a teacher
- Unexcused absences, sporadic but persistent
- Unexcused tardies that show a pattern of disregard for your class

When students consistently miss or come late to class:

1. Find out why they are coming late or missing school as the reasons are often, though not always, connected to larger issues of family difficulties, poverty, or health problems.

2. Prevent the problem of absenteeism or tardiness by establishing clear expectations regarding attendance through your syllabus and your *actions* in the opening weeks.

3. Set the standard yourself: be in class on time and ready to go at the bell yourself.

4. Begin with an activity that makes the start of class important and imposes a consequence if missed: a quiz or a writing or reading assignment for the first five or ten minutes, which students cannot make up if they are not present.

5. Keep accurate attendance records—for *all* students—so you can make them aware of the pattern and have the evidence for subsequent administrative follow-up.

6. Meet with the student at the first sign of any pattern of absence or tardiness to develop both an understanding of the problem and a plan to avoid the problem in the future.

7. Communicate to students the consequences for their reputation and their grade if they persist in coming late or missing class.

8. Avoid humiliating students who enter late or are frequently absent; instead, talk to them later to find out the reason and clarify for them the cost of their actions.

9. Contact parents if your efforts prove futile. Convey to them in an objective, professional tone your concern, what you have tried so far, the cost of their child's actions, and the scale of the problem.

10. Follow all school policies regarding attendance as they relate to making up quizzes, tests, and assignments.

3. Record Keeping

Record keeping serves many legal, instructional, and administrative purposes. Keep, organize, and store for easy access the following:

- **Health Information:** procedures and problems for specific students

- **Special Education Information:** accommodations and other procedures

- **Procedural Information:** maps, codes, routes, drills, calendars, and essential contact information in case of an emergency

- **Attendance:** roll sheets, attendance rosters, attendance reports

- **Assessment Data:** passwords, access codes, or user names for all online data access; reading and other testing data about students' performance in academic areas; grades and performance data on such assessments as Advanced Placement exams and state exit exams

- **Documentation:** any data you keep on participation, behavior, or infractions

- **Handouts and Lesson Plans:** extra copies for those who were absent when you passed them out

To avoid legal, administrative, or instructional problems related to information:

1. Keep a binder or clipboard (preferably with a storage space) at hand with essential emergency medical information, special education accommodations, and reading scores. This information should be secure but easily referenced.

2. Have emergency escape routes, procedures, and contact information readily available in the event of a crisis.

AthleStock/Index Open

3. Maintain accurate, up-to-date records of attendance, as well as any summary reports for attendance or progress reports.

4. Store any information relating to grades, attendance, or students in a secure place where students cannot access it; if it is stored online or on a computer in your room, be sure it is password protected.

5. Organize all vital data, especially your class rosters, in one place—e.g., the clipboard or binder you use for other information—for quick retrieval in the event of an evacuation. It is vital that you bring that information to account for and protect those students who may have medical or psychiatric conditions.

6. Make copies of seating charts to use for record keeping purposes such as participation in discussions, group assignments, and accommodations to consider in placement.

7. Back up all essential student information, such as grades and rosters, and keep in a separate place to prevent loss.

8. Create a "Student Information Form" to help you gather essential, current information about your students' needs, contact information, interests, and suggestions about how you can help them learn and succeed in your class.

9. Consider requiring students to keep track of their own grades for the class as a backup and opportunity to teach them to monitor their own academic standing.

10. Designate a place to keep extra copies of handouts, announcements, and your lesson plans from previous days for easy reference when students return from being absent.

4. Abuse

Abuse within the classroom takes several forms, not all of which are easily witnessed in a larger class:

- **Sexual:** Touching, speaking, or otherwise acting in any inappropriate way with sexual intent.

- **Physical:** touching another with intent to harm or intimidate.

- **Verbal:** speaking words to another with intent to offend, injure, or coerce.

- **Emotional:** using any combination of means including gestures, actions, or words intended to upset or harm.

Prevent or respond to any form of abuse in one or more of these ways:

1. Emphasize from the first day of class that this is a safe environment where no abuse of any form will be tolerated.

2. Clarify for students, if necessary, what behavior is inappropriate and the consequences of such behavior; be consistent in your enforcement of these standards.

3. Monitor mounting tensions between students and intervene before they act upon them. Clarify the source of the tension and move to resolve it immediately. If it becomes necessary to send students out of the room, request an administrative escort. Do *not* send the students together or separately, as one may await the other and then assault them in the hall, as no one is likely to be around.

4. Meet with students you suspect or know are being abused, are abusing others, or may be injuring themselves to discuss the best way to handle the problem. Emphasize that the behavior cannot be allowed to continue, that you are concerned about them and wish to help. Listen to what they have to say, then tell them that you intend to talk to their counselor or, in more severe cases, the administration, because your job is to ensure that all students in your class are safe.

5. Confront students who engage in bullying behavior immediately but privately. What you see in class may only be part of a larger pattern of abuse outside the class.

6. Document any incidents of abuse—date, time, people involved, what was said or done—and include these in any communication with counselors, administration, or others involved.

7. Consult the administration regarding any students in your class who have a history of violence; most states require schools to inform teachers if a student is on parole for violent behavior. Tragedies in recent years have taught us to take all threatening speech seriously; immediately report any threats to harm you or any students. Likewise, students who include violent themes in written work or art projects should be referred to the counselor, who should have the work sample.

8. Call students on offensive language; reiterate the class policies. If they say, "I was just kidding," confront them about this, emphasizing that there is no such thing in your class. Teach them to accept responsibility for their words and actions.

9. Insist on a behavior contract, a meeting with the students, or both before allowing them to return to class after a violent incident in the class. Confirm with the administration that this contract is appropriate and to be sure they know about its terms in the event that you must enforce it.

10. Get help immediately if a serious fight breaks out that you are unable to stop right away. Send specific students to get help if necessary, as opposed to saying to the class in general, "Someone go get help!" Do *not* leave the classroom where the fight is taking place. The laws are very complicated about whether you should actively try to break up a fight, offering seemingly contradictory

messages that suggest you should intervene because you will be responsible for harm done, while also implying that if you do get involved and harm or are harmed by a student, you could be held liable. In short, protect those not involved and move decisively to get the help needed to break up the fight and thus protect those involved from serious injury.

5. Cheating

> **Problems to Watch For:**
>
> • Homework, papers, or tests copied from classmates, friends, or siblings who took the same course
>
> • Plagiarism from uncited sources, most notably the Internet
>
> • Purchased papers from online sites that sell them
>
> • Cheating on exams

Thanks to the Internet and other tech gadgets, cheating is a more common problem than ever. Consider the following ways to prevent or respond to cheating:

1. Define what constitutes cheating or plagiarism in your class.

2. Communicate and post your policies on cheating as well as those of the administration. If your policies differ from the administration, make sure you will have administrative support if you try to carry them through.

3. Create assignments that make cheating impossible. If you ask students to write a paper about the subject of nature in Robert Frost's poems, you can be sure some will find papers on the Internet and borrow heavily or merely copy the whole thing.

4. Confront a student you suspect of cheating, but be sure to have evidence for your allegation. If, for example, you find the material online, print out a copy and attach it to the student's paper discretely. Never let a student off without a consequence for such an offense. Also, seek to understand why the student

cheated; there may be something in his or her remarks that teaches you something of use for the future.

5. Clarify the difference between collaborating and cheating in general or on a specific assignment. Some students come from cultures where it is not only considered appropriate to share answers but encouraged.

6. Request that students clear their desk of any materials but those appropriate for the exam they will take.

7. Monitor the room during any testing, asking students to store books, bags, or binders as needed if they appear to be a possible source of cheating.

8. Provide different versions of multiple choice tests and alternate them accordingly so students are not surrounded by copies of the same exam and thus enticed to cheat.

9. Be clear about expected behavior during a test: no talking, no moving around, approaching only you if they have questions.

10. Avoid humiliating students in front of others if you determine they have cheated. Follow up any such discovery by informing the student's counselor, the administration, and the student's parents.

6. Materials and Equipment

> **Problems to Watch For:**
>
> In an era of expensive textbooks, fragile and costly technology, and large classes, it is part of your job as teacher to prevent destruction, loss, or damage of:
>
> - Materials such as textbooks, supplies for art, science labs, or shop class
> - Equipment for science labs, woodshop, computer classes
> - Other resources like projectors, DVD/CD players, stereos, Smartboards, printers, or televisions

To prevent or address problems with the use or abuse of school resources:

1. Pay attention to the environment in which students are working by moving around from station to station, group to group.

2. Check out material to specific students, making them personally responsible for the textbook, the microscope, computer, or supplies. Remind them that the materials are checked out under their name and that they are thus responsible for them.

3. Stay in the workspace at all times.

4. Explain the cost and consequence of vandalism both to themselves, and to all students in general (e.g., diminished resources, lack of access due to increased security, lack of trust).

5. Keep cleaning supplies handy to remove graffiti right away.

6. Require students to cover textbooks and determine the precise condition of the book at the time they checked it out.

7. Document—in writing, by photograph, or by photocopy—what the student did if possible; submit this evidence to the administration along with your report. This is especially important in the

case of "tagging" (i.e., graffiti), as many schools create a book of such students' "tags" so they can identify them in the future.

8. Avoid checking out to students equipment they could not afford to replace such as a laptops, projectors, graphic calculators, or other expensive items the school itself would struggle to replace.

9. Store equipment, materials, and supplies in safe places where students cannot easily access or vandalize them.

10. Meet with the student about an incident, discussing the consequences and cost; in accordance with school policies, you can then follow up with the administration or the student's parents.

7. Field Trips

> **Problems to Watch For:**
>
> Taking a large group of students anywhere poses challenges and causes problems that can have legal, logistical, or administrative consequences. Examples of such class trips include:
>
> - The library for research
> - Labs for experiments
> - The auditorium for performances, rallies, or assemblies
> - Off-campus trips

To assure all class outings are successful and safe:

1. Review where you are going, how you will go there, and why.

2. Establish clear expectations for what to bring and how to act.

3. Discuss specific rules before and upon arriving at the computer lab, media center, library, or off-campus location.

4. Bring along your roster and any appropriate emergency information you might need. This might include procedural or contact information in the event of a medical emergency.

5. Talk to individual students ahead of time if they have misbehaved in similar situations, emphasizing what you expect and getting from them a promise that they will behave.

6. Remind students when you arrive at the location what they are expected to do while there, and what to do if they should get lost or have a problem. Reiterate to them that they are not to go off on their own to sit with friends in the auditorium, separate from the group at the museum, or course work.

7. Monitor students' progress on any work in the library or other location so you can tell students when to start saving, printing, or putting away their work or the equipment and materials.

8. Follow all regulations when traveling off campus with students, including transportation codes and adult-to-student ratios.

9. Check ahead of time with the librarian, lab assistant, or contact person at the off-campus site to make sure that everything is confirmed and ready to go on the designated date.

10. Bring with you any materials, handouts, supplies, or equipment students might need at the site so you can be sure the event will be a success.

8. Substitutes

Problems to Watch For:

- Students disrupt the class and prevent people from working
- Students disrespect the substitute
- Substitutes undermine the class by not following directions

Ensure a safe and productive class when a substitute comes by doing the following:

1. Choose, if possible, a substitute you know you can trust to manage the class effectively and execute your lesson plan as directed. If you know ahead of time you will be absent, book the substitute in advance. It is sometimes possible to develop an ongoing relationship with a sub; this has the advantage of providing consistency for the students when you are away.

2. Provide all the materials your substitute will need to run the class. Do not expect the sub to make photocopies, secure equipment, or otherwise gather up the necessary supplies.

3. Tell your students you will be out—if you know ahead of time—so you can go over what they will do and what you expect. Assure them that you have done everything you can to make sure that the class will run smoothly.

4. Include with your lesson plans specific details about which classes your substitute will teach and where.

5. Give the substitute a photocopy of your class roster and the attendance sheet. It is essential that the sub also has an up-to-date seating chart. Other useful items to provide include a copy of the bell schedule, names of helpful students, a copy of your policies, and copies of referral forms in the event that the substitute must send students to the office for causing trouble.

6. Add to your lesson plan any specific instructions about things like collecting student work or allowing students with special needs to work in certain ways.

7. Set up an emergency substitute folder in the event that you should ever be out unexpectedly for a day or two. These would be engaging activities any sub could use to keep the students working well until you return or new instructions arrive.

8. Assume that meaningful instruction and work can happen while you are away instead of assuming they'll just have a baby sitter. There is nothing wrong with asking the substitute to show a clip from a video, but that doesn't mean she has to let it run the whole period.

9. Be clear in your instructions about not only what you want students to do but how you want them to work (e.g., quietly on their own or in groups) during the period.

10. Follow up when you return, using the substitute's report to evaluate how things went so you can praise students for what they did well and focus on what they need to do better next time. Keep in mind for next time—though you should not be taking too many days away from your classes—what went wrong and plan some new way to avoid that problem.

9. Emergencies

> **Problems to Watch For:**
>
> Sadly, as teachers we now face the possibility of many different emergencies depending on who and where we teach. These crises fall into different categories:
>
> - Medical: asthma, food allergies (e.g., peanuts), and more
> - Mental: bipolar, depression, suicide, cutting, and traumatic responses to certain subjects or images (e.g., I had a student who, upon hearing the word "blood" or seeing blood in a film, would pass out.)
> - Environmental: toxic materials on or around the campus
> - Natural: fire, earthquake, hurricane, tornado, flooding
> - Terrorist: weapons, explosives, and other hazardous substances used by students, adults, or actual terrorists

Ensure the safety of all students by following these guidelines regarding such emergencies:

1. Store any medical supplies provided by the school or the family of a student with allergies in a place you can reach immediately.

2. Assign specific students particular roles in a time of crisis so you know things will get done immediately.

3. Maintain your calm during any crisis: your fear will spread to students, so it is your job to set the tone.

4. Take all emergency drills seriously; ask students to do the same, pointing out that those who pay attention to the flight attendants' instructions survive in-flight emergencies at higher rates than those who don't.

5. Post and review all evacuation plans, as well as plans for other types of crises, such as a bomb threat, intruder, or earthquakes.

6. Bring your roll book as well as appropriate emergency supplies or information when leaving the classroom to go to a designated evacuation spot.

7. During any emergency, issue clear, direct instructions about what to do, where to be, what to watch for, and what to expect.

8. Follow all appropriate procedures for the emergency you are experiencing as each one is designed to protect the students.

9. Monitor students closely to make sure they stay where they are supposed to; remind them that their parents will expect them to be at school in an emergency.

10. Appoint responsible students to do certain tasks, such as taking roll, while you move among your students to keep them calm or assess their condition.

10. Conferences

Depending on the purpose and situation, a conference concerning a student might include:

- Parents
- The student
- Administrators
- Counselors
- Teachers
- Specialists (e.g., school psychologists, speech therapists, reading specialists)
- Parole officers or school safety advocates
- Legal counsel
- District officials

When attending or calling for any conferences regarding a student:

1. Treat parents as partners, members of a team that exists to help this student succeed in life.

2. Prepare yourself and any others for the conference if you initiated it. Give them a general sense of the purpose for the meeting, and make clear where and when it will be. If it is appropriate

Cindy Charles/PhotoEdit

to provide documentation or materials to review prior to the meeting, get those to the interested parties as early as possible with specific instructions about what to do with them.

3. Understand that some parents, owing to their own difficulties in school, find such meetings very intimidating and difficult. They may have assumptions about school, teachers, or administrators that color their perspective.

4. Speak about the child with respect and concern, whether she is there or not. Criticizing a child in front of a parent is a sure way to undermine the effectiveness of the meeting.

5. Meet ahead of time with other support staff if appropriate to insure the meeting is successful. This might mean going over certain aspects of a student's performance or behavior with the psychologist or safety advocate to make sure you both understand what the meeting will try to accomplish and how you can each work to achieve that result.

6. Focus on observable actions when discussing students instead of characterizing them as "a bully" or "having a terrible attitude." An objective tone will help establish and maintain a more professional, measured tone in the meeting instead of upsetting the parent who may hear a teacher's words as biased.

7. Document your concerns, bringing any test data, grades, or evidence of work that would help the discussion.

8. Seek the help of a colleague, such as a counselor, to facilitate a meeting between you and a student or you, the student, and the parents if you feel it would be beneficial to have a third party there.

9. Consider whether it is appropriate or safe to meet with students individually. Often it is better to arrange the meeting in the library or some other public place; if you do meet in your class, keep the door open and tell a colleague what you are doing.

10. Enter into the meeting with a clear sense of what you want to accomplish and how your actions are in the best interest of the student. Bring whatever information or resources will help you achieve that result. Appear at all times to be motivated by your concern for your student's personal and educational well-being.

Recommended Resources and Reading

The following books proved essential in writing this book. They go into much more detail about the ideas I've included, as well as others I did not have space to include or that might be helpful but did not seem so essential.

Costa, A. L. (Ed.). (2001). *Developing minds: A resource book for teaching thinking*. Alexandria, VA: Association for Supervision and Curriculum Development.

Costa, A. L., & Garmston, R. J. (2002). *Cognitive coaching: A foundation for renaissance schools*. Norwood, MA: Christopher-Gordon.

Curwin, R. L., & Mendler, A. N. (1999). *Discipline with dignity*. Upper Saddle River, NJ: Merrill Prentice Hall.

Echevarria, J., & Graves, A. (2003). *Sheltered content instruction: Teaching English-language learners with diverse abilities*. Boston: Allyn and Bacon.

Emmer, E. T., Evertson, C. E., & Worsham, M. E. (2006). *Classroom management for middle and high school teachers*. Boston: Pearson.

Gardner, H. (1999). *The disciplined mind: What all students should understand*. New York: Simon and Schuster.

Jones, F. H. (1987). *Positive classroom discipline*. New York: McGraw-Hill.

Kohn, A. (2006). *Beyond discipline: From compliance to community*. Alexandria, VA: Association for Supervision and Curriculum Development.

Marzano, R. J., Marzano, J. S., & Pickering, D. J. (2003). *Classroom management that works: Researched-based strategies for every teacher*. Alexandria, VA: Association for Supervision and Curriculum Development.

National Research Council. (2000). *How people learn: Brain, mind, experience, and school*. Washington, DC: National Academy Press.

Schoenbach, R., Greenleaf, C., Cziko, C., & Hurwitz, L. (1999). *Reading for understanding: A guide to improving reading in middle and high school classrooms*. San Francisco: Jossey-Bass.

Slavin, R. E. (2006). *Educational psychology: Theory and practice*. Boston: Pearson.

Smith, M. W., & Wilhelm, J. D. (2002). *"Reading don't fix no chevys": Literacy in the lives of young men*. Portsmouth, NH: Heinemann.

Sprick, R. S. (1985). *Discipline in the secondary classroom: A problem-by-problem survival guide*. San Francisco: Jossey-Bass.

Sterrett, E. A. (2000). *The manager's pocket guide© to emotional intelligence*. Amherst, MA: HRD Press.

Thompson, J. G. (1998). *Discipline survival kit for the secondary teacher*. San Francisco: Jossey-Bass.

Wong, H. K., & Wong, R. T. (1988). *The first days of school*. Mountain View, CA: Harry K. Wong Publications.